Overview

A sales transaction is a frontline interface between a seller and a customer. From the moment the sale is agreed, the process is very much a single action involving the salesperson. However, getting to this point involves the combined efforts of many people in the organization and the full support of the Sales and Marketing Departments.

The sales and marketing functions have a symbiotic relationship, as the activities of both are interdependent and mutually beneficial. There's no point in marketing a product if there isn't a sales function to do the actual selling. Likewise, it's almost impossible to successfully sell a product without marketing planning and support.

Sales is a difficult discipline to master. There are no quick solutions that can guarantee sales success. In today's ever-shifting, globally competitive environment, achieving success in sales is harder than ever.

This course discusses the close connection between sales and marketing. In addition, it details key competencies that can benefit a sales professional. It also covers trends that influence the current sales environment and how these have changed the buyer-seller relationship. This course will also give insight into consumer buying behavior, the buying decision process, and the sales process.

With increasing competition in a global economy, it's essential to have a good sales strategy. Strategic sales planning helps you understand the needs of your customers, which leads to increased revenue and improved client loyalty. It also helps to shorten the sales cycle and allows you to identify and take advantage of the best opportunities.

In this course, you'll learn about the four steps of developing a sales strategy.

The first step is analyzing the competition, which allows you to understand your company's place in the marketplace.

The next step is segmenting customers, which helps you understand how to group together customers who have similar purchasing desires, needs, challenges, and price sensitivities.

The third step is to create clear, concise, and feasible value propositions, which explain to customers the benefit of buying or using your products or services. In the last step, you'll learn how to develop a sales process, which defines what sales activities to undertake, and when. The topics in this course are structured to take you through the

Sales Foundation

steps, and the final topic allows you to demonstrate your knowledge as you put all the steps together.

Are you a person who thinks salespeople are born and not made? Well, it's true that some people seem born to sell, but most others have to learn how. Learning how to sell anything can be frightening – the potential for failure is high. However, there are techniques that can make the process of pitching, negotiating, and closing a sale much easier.

In this course, you'll learn about activities that are done in steps four, five, and six of the sales process – presenting, discovering, and closing.

You'll learn how to prepare and deliver effective sales presentations. This includes organizing content according to the structure of a typical sales presentation, and rehearsing with a coach.

Next, you'll learn about how to prepare for a negotiation. You'll learn about the four main types of objections and how to counter them. And then you'll learn how to negotiate a sale.

Finally, the course will show you how to close a sale by building momentum, recognizing when to close, and choosing the closing methods that are appropriate for you, your customers, and your sales situation.

Sorin Dumitrascu

A sale is a transaction that takes place between two parties. It can involve a selling organization and a buying organization, or a salesperson and a customer. For this transaction to be successful there is one fundamental requirement: respect.

If you don't consider respect the cornerstone of a strong customer relationship, you will find it hard to make the sale. A sale that is negotiated without mutual respect between the two parties could easily fall through.

To build respect you must get to know your customer.

This course describes the different types of customers that you may encounter and demonstrates how to get to know them.

This course also explains the importance of being able to communicate effectively with customers.

You will learn about the guidelines for communicating in a sales meeting and how to apply them in your own work.

During this course, you will learn how to forge strong relationships with customers through effective communication. You will also learn about the concept of sales credibility and how to build credibility with your prospective customers. In an ever-changing and highly-competitive sales environment, credibility can help you stand out from the crowd and consistently achieve successful sales.

A culture is a set of characteristics that distinguishes one group of people from another, and that is shared and reinforced by members within that group. The tendencies of individuals within a culture to share characteristics and behaviors are called cultural predispositions.

An organization's business culture is the unique pattern of behavior, knowledge, and purpose that makes it unique. It defines what's valued, respected, and rewarded within an organization.

People within a business culture have a set of shared attitudes, assumptions, and practices that characterize the organization and differentiate it from other businesses. These principles guide the actions of employees in working toward corporate goals and meeting organizational expectations.

There are often subcultures within a business culture that define how a department or function, such as sales, operates within and relates to the organization as a whole. Understanding how sales cultures work can help you excel within them.

In this course, you'll learn about the five

different types of sales cultures and how alignment influences the effectiveness of the sales function. You'll also discover the importance of your own sales culture and how it influences your overall sales effectiveness.

Have you ever been on either side of a situation like this? Juan is shopping for a new computer. A salesperson tries to help by reciting all the product features and specifications of the various choices. At one point, Juan's eyes glaze over. He becomes overwhelmed by too much technical data, and he leaves the store empty-handed. Perhaps if the salesperson had used customer-focused selling, this scenario might have ended with a sale and a happy customer.

In a customer-focused sales approach, you find out what customers want or need, and provide the solution for their specific situations. Using this approach, you can increase sales, profits, and customer loyalty. You can compete on value instead of price, and create competitive barriers to entry. In this course, you'll learn about the benefits of customer-focused selling and the barriers you may encounter when implementing it.

You'll also learn about the five main principles of customer-focused selling. These include talking

Sales Foundation

situationally with customers, not just giving presentations, and asking relevant questions instead of giving opinions about what they should purchase.

The principles also include focusing on the solution and not on your relationship with the buyer, and discussing the product's usage without trying to sell only its features. Also, you'll learn how to close on the buyer's time frame, not the seller's.

In this course, you'll also have an opportunity to practice using some of the principles of customer-focused selling, which will help your customers see you as a consultant, not as a "pushy salesperson." You'll also learn about customer relationship management – also known as CRM – which is a strategy used to learn more about customers' needs and behaviors in order to develop stronger relationships with them.

CHAPTER 1 - Introduction to Sales
Sales Versus Marketing: What is the Difference?
Effective Sales: Competencies and Trends
Buyer Behavior
An Introduction to the Sales Process

Sales Versus Marketing: What is the Difference?

Sales and marketing are closely linked functions, and sometimes they can overlap. Some experts believe that sales should be incorporated entirely into the marketing function, while others claim that sales should be a standalone function. Either way, it's important for both Sales and Marketing Departments to communicate and collaborate closely together.

The roles of sales and marketing can vary from one organization to another. Generally though, the role of sales involves setting up accounts and generating sales, dealing with front line customers, and building business relationships. And the role of marketing entails generating leads for sales, branding and messaging, and long-term planning.

The sales function in an organization

Company executives are often very confident about their products, and will sometimes say that a product is so good, it sells itself. While the product in question may be good, as a rule, all products need a sales workforce to sell them.

The main function of an organization's Sales Department is to attract and retain customers.

The Sales Department needs to ensure it meets customer demand. To do this, the department hires salespeople or outside agencies to carry out the necessary sales activities.

Salespeople must also analyze market demands. To do this, they need to understand the psychology of the target customer, anticipate and react accordingly to market fluctuations, and explore the possibility of new markets.

In addition to making the all-important sale, each salesperson should be aware of the need for business development – creating new business opportunities for the organization. Pursuing new business opportunities helps salespeople develop new business relationships. These relationships can help generate increased sales as well as position the salesperson and the organization for future success.

Sales Foundation

Question

Based on what you've learned so far, what do you think are the main functions of an organization's Sales Department?

Options:

1. To attract customers
2. To retain customers
3. To deal with customer complaints
4. To process customer orders

Answer

Option 1: This option is correct. Attracting customers is one of the core tenets for a Sales Department. This is an important revenue-creating function.

Option 2: This option is correct. Retaining customers is an essential function for those working in Sales Departments. Retaining customers ensures that a revenue stream is created and sustained.

Option 3: This option is incorrect. Dealing with customer complaints is a function of the Customer Service Department. Employees in the Sales Department should be allowed to concentrate on sales and business development.

Option 4: This option is incorrect. Processing customer orders is a function of the Customer Service Department. Salespeople should be concentrating on selling and developing new business opportunities.

There are many different opinions on where the sales function should be located in a corporate structure. Some organizations favor having sales work in tandem with the marketing function, while others prefer to keep sales as a standalone function.

There are arguments for and against both options. But no matter how the organization is structured with regard to the marketing and sales functions, it's imperative that the groups maintain regular communication with each other.

In fact, the Sales Department should establish close ties with nearly every section of an organization, including Research and Development (R&D), Human Resources, Manufacturing, Finance, and Customer Service.

Each organization has its own unique sales system. But these systems are affected by several common forces:

- external forces,
- corporate strategy, and
- marketing and sales strategies.

The first type of force is external forces, which range from issues concerning competition and customers to environmental factors. These forces can represent an opportunity or a threat, depending

Sales Foundation

on the organization. For example, very cold weather is good for a company that sells thermal underwear, but not for a company that sells suntan lotion.

The second force that can affect the sales system is the corporate strategy. The way a company organizes its business goals and objectives will directly affect sales.

The final force, marketing and sales strategies, identifies potential customers and dictates how the selling is to be carried out. Both the Marketing and Sales Departments are responsible for deciding on market segmentation and product and service offerings.

The roles of sales and marketing

Companies rely on sales to generate income. Whether the product is tangible, like a laptop computer, or intangible, like an insurance policy, it needs to be sold.

Sales is linked to marketing. It is the Marketing Department's responsibility to create the image and identify the market for the product.

Sales is used to communicate the image that marketing has created for the product. The Sales Department will take the product and sell it to the market. The sales pitch will emphasize that this is the right product, at the right time and price, and in the right place.

The roles of sales and marketing can differ greatly depending on the organization and the type of product it's selling. For instance, if a company is selling magazine subscriptions, it's less likely to require field sales representatives. Sales of the service would be more marketing-oriented and based on direct mail, Web-based advertising, and TV, radio, and print advertising.

However if the company was selling a new pharmaceutical product, it might have more of an emphasis on sales. Direct marketing might be less effective for this type of product.

Sales Foundation

Organizations are often said to be either sales or marketing focused, based on which function has the larger budget. Examples of sales organizations are pharmaceutical companies and consultancy companies, while marketing organizations can include consumer product companies and travel and leisure companies.

Many Sales and Marketing Departments interact closely and frequently. After all, they have the same single goal – to get customers to buy the product. It's up to the Marketing Department to create a coherent strategy to sell the product, then the Sales Department will have to do the actual selling.

Question

In the Sales Department of your own organization, how much emphasis do you think is placed on developing a rapport with customers?

Options:

1. Highly emphasized
2. Occasionally encouraged
3. Not considered to be essential

Answer

Option 1: You say that your Sales Department places a high emphasis on developing a rapport with customers. This is an excellent way of generating repeat sales.

Option 2: You've indicated that your Sales Department only occasionally encourages the development of a rapport with customers. Perhaps the Sales Department should concentrate on this aspect of its selling technique in order to increase sales.

Option 3: You've said that in your Sales Department, developing a rapport with customers is not considered to be essential. Establishing close ties with customers can generate repeat sales. Your organization may want to reconsider its approach.

Though Marketing and Sales are closely linked, both departments have separate responsibilities. The role of sales involves setting up accounts and generating sales, dealing with front line customers, and building business relationships.

Setting up accounts and generating sales

Salespeople set up accounts for customers in order to track activity and help facilitate repeat sales. These accounts also often involve a preferred customer discount or other incentives to increase account sales.

Dealing with front line customers

Salespeople deal with an organization's front line customers regularly. This involves working with both potential and existing customers and is useful for providing customer feedback to the Marketing Department.

Building business relationships

Salespeople have to nurture and build business relationships. They do this by communicating with existing and prospective customers, anticipating their needs, and selling them the right products.

The role of marketing consists of different tasks than sales. Marketing involves generating leads for sales, branding and messaging, and long–term planning.

Generating leads for sales

When marketing staff carry out research in advance of launching a new product, or rebranding an old one, they may encounter leads which could generate future sales. They would typically pass these leads on to their colleagues in the Sales Department.

Branding and messaging

Marketers are responsible for developing a strategy that will help the product sell. This includes developing and implementing branding and messaging strategies for the product.

Long-term planning

Sorin Dumitrascu

Marketers take a strategic, long-term planning approach. They determine how to communicate a product's marketing message to the relevant demographic.

Question

Match the department with the roles its staff members carry out. Each department may match to more than one role.

Options:

A. Sales Department
B. Marketing Department

Targets:

1. Setting up accounts
2. Dealing with front line customers
3. Building business relationships
4. Generating leads for sales
5. Branding and messaging
6. Long-term planning

Answer

Setting up accounts and generating sales is a core activity for the Sales Department.

Dealing with front line customers is a task that employees in the Sales Department carry out on a daily basis.

Building business relationships is a key way for staff in the Sales Department to generate new as

Sales Foundation

well as repeat sales.

Generating leads for sales is something staff members in the Marketing Department do as they research different market opportunities.

Branding and messaging products is the Marketing Department's responsibility.

Long-term planning is carried out by the Marketing Department as its staff members decide what markets products should be targeted at.

Effective Sales: Competencies and Trends

Successful salespeople must solve problems and provide the right solutions for their customers. They also need to influence customers' buying decisions so that a product gets sold.

There are certain key competencies that, if mastered, can prove very beneficial for a career in sales. These competencies include being able to communicate effectively, possessing the necessary selling knowledge and skills, having adequate knowledge of customer and product, having the necessary sales management and support skills, and being able to plan strategically.

There are four main trends that affect the sales environment. They are technological advances, the global marketplace, a diverse workforce, and increased competition.

These trends have affected the buyer-seller relationship in several ways. These include increased seller cooperation, an emphasis on relationship selling, a focus on seller responsiveness, and an enhanced scope for productivity.

Sales roles and responsibilities

The sales environment encompasses many different roles. These roles can vary in complexity and in the range of responsibilities that go with them. Successful salespeople must solve problems and provide the right solutions for customers. They also need to influence a customer's buying decisions so that a product gets sold. In addition, they need to facilitate profitable buying strategies by understanding the market they're selling into.

Though a salesperson's responsibilities will vary from one organization to another, these responsibilities can be classified as either direct or indirect.

One of the first tasks a salesperson must deal with is direct selling responsibilities. These affect how the salesperson will initiate the sales process and how face-to-face encounters with customers are handled.

Some examples of direct selling responsibilities include looking for prospective customers, building relationships, attracting customer interest, and discovering customer needs.

Indirect selling responsibilities involve the tasks a salesperson must carry out in preparation for making a sale, such as pleasing customers, and seeking repeat sales.

This type of responsibility is more time consuming than direct selling responsibilities, as it often involves providing extended services for the customer.

Examples of indirect selling responsibilities include: handling complaints, maintaining customer relations, collecting accounts, and networking.

To gain a better understanding of the different roles and responsibilities involved in sales, consider three examples of distinct sales roles: an account manager, a call center supervisor, and a sales administrator. Each role represents a different level of authority and responsibility.

An account manager with a software development company is in charge of generating sales from a portfolio of accounts. The account manager works toward agreed targets and tries to maximize profitability as much as possible. The account manager's responsibilities also include identifying new customers, monitoring customer feedback, and keeping track of competitors. Being aware of new developments in sales generation and product development is another vital responsibility.

A call center supervisor for an insurance company oversees the employees of the call center

Sales Foundation

to make sure that they make effective sales calls. The supervisor allocates work in the call center so that it's evenly distributed. This role requires that service levels be continually monitored. The supervisor also has to maintain records of activity levels, and investigate and resolve any problems that may arise.

A sales administrator working for a clothing manufacturer processes customer orders and makes sure that customers receive the correct goods on the agreed delivery dates and for the correct prices. The administrator needs to maintain regular contact with customers to inform them of the progress of their orders. In addition, this role requires the administrator to keep accurate and up-to-date records on stock and delivery details.

Question

Match the type of sales responsibility to the corresponding example. Each responsibility may match to more than one example.

Options:

A. Direct selling responsibility
B. Indirect selling responsibility

Targets:

1. A salesperson reads the business section of the newspaper to search for potential new customers

2. By regularly attending industry conferences, a salesperson gains insight into what customers might want from a product

3. A salesperson arranges to meet with a customer who isn't happy with a product

4. A salesperson meets different industry representatives at a trade show and gathers contacts

Answer

One example of a direct selling responsibility is when a salesperson searches for prospective customers.

An example of a direct selling responsibility is when a salesperson uncovers the potential needs of a customer.

A salesperson meeting with an unhappy customer is an example of an indirect selling responsibility. The salesperson is handling the customer's complaint.

The salesperson using the trade show as an opportunity to network is an example of an indirect selling responsibility.

Sales competencies and expectations

The complex and often pressurized sales environment can be a harsh place for employees. However, there are certain key competencies that, if mastered, can prove to be very beneficial for a career in sales.

In fact, many sales experts believe that these selling-oriented competencies should be expected of everyone involved in sales, from sales administrators to account managers, regardless of their roles.

There are five competency areas that can help professional salespeople do their jobs effectively: being able to communicate effectively with others

having broad selling skills and knowledge

having a good basis of knowledge about the customer and product possessing skills in sales management and support, and

having the ability to plan strategically

The first competency, being able to communicate effectively, is a fundamental requirement in sales. Effective communication means the salesperson can articulate recommendations, sales approach, and strategy in a clear and persuasive way to customers and other key stakeholders.

Sorin Dumitrascu

A salesperson needs to communicate the validity of the sales pitch. When in discussion with potential customers, it needs to be made clear that the salesperson's company has the ability to deliver. Clear communication can lead to increased sales.

For example, a company provides elocution lessons for its salespeople so that they can become more confident in their ability to communicate effectively with customers. As a result the company sees a noticeable increase in sales in the following quarter.

The second competency, having broad selling skills and knowledge, involves the salesperson being aware of the latest developments in sales techniques and trends. This competency is a prerequisite for selling professionally and effectively in competitive markets. If a company's salespeople becomes more confident and polished in their approach, they'll be better able to convince customers of the superiority of the product they're selling. For instance, many companies require their salespeople to attend seminars delivered by sales experts.

Knowing your customer and product is the third competency. Efficient salespeople research potential customers to understand their needs and match them with products to provide solutions.

Sales Foundation

Salespeople must explain the benefits of the product they're selling in detail. They must know the limits of the product and the application to which it's most suited. They have to be extremely familiar with the product's special features and functions so that they can outline the advantages the product can deliver to the customer.

Consider this example. A salesperson for a coolant manufacturer learns from a trade journal that an aerospace firm is experiencing overheating problems with its new engine. The salesperson contacts the company and explains the merits of the coolant and arranges a trial. The trial proves successful and a lucrative contract is signed.

Question

Which of the examples demonstrates effective use of communication to increase sales?

Options:

1. A salesperson writes a new sales pitch for a product
2. A salesperson uses a previously existing sales pitch for a new product, but changes the details where necessary
3. A salesperson doesn't write a sales pitch, and improvises instead

Answer

Option 1: This is the correct option. By writing a new sales pitch for the product, the salesperson is using effective communication by bringing a fresh, concentrated approach to the task.

Option 2: This option is incorrect. By using an existing sales pitch, the salesperson is not using effective communication. The old pitch might be stale, and it hasn't been tailored to the product in question.

Option 3: This option is incorrect. By not writing a sales pitch and relying on improvisation instead, the salesperson is running the risk of forgetting some important information about the product, or worse, mistakenly claiming the product can do something it can't.

The fourth competency, possessing sales management and support skills, brings focus to the selling process and greatly enhances the chance of achieving targets.

This competency involves the use of technology to generate sales reports, forecast future sales, and manage other sales-related processes. By adopting a management-led approach to the selling process, a salesperson can clearly establish goals and efficiently work toward accomplishing them.

For example, a salesperson working for a PC

manufacturer uses office management techniques to organize the administrative tasks associated with the role. Relieving this administrative burden allows the salesperson to achieve greater time efficiency. This means that there's now more time available to concentrate on finding and talking to prospective customers.

The final competency, being able to plan strategically, requires the salesperson to have a strong

understanding of the organization's corporate strategy. This competency involves the ability to tie long- term vision into short-term goals.

To become competent at strategic planning, a salesperson must collaborate with other individuals in the Sales Department to create a strategy-based approach to selling. This involves creating a sales message that targeted customers will find appealing and respond to.

For example, a medical device manufacturing company's sales force identifies ten hospitals with the largest purchasing budgets and creates a schedule to target each hospital at a separate time during the year.

Question

Match the key competencies to the examples of

how they contribute to sales success.

Options:

A. Being able to communicate effectively

B. Having broad selling skills and knowledge

C. Knowing your customer and product

D. Possessing sales management and support skills

E. Being able to plan strategically

Targets:

1. A stationery company's salespeople ensures their sales pitches are coherent and aligned, resulting in a spike in sales

2. By using the latest e-sales techniques, an online T-shirt company's sales increase

3. A pesticide salesperson targets a product for killing insects to customers in areas where crops are being destroyed by insects

4. A salesman's commission increases after he modernizes his filing system

5. A company increases profits by pushing sales when its competitor's stock is low

Answer

Ensuring that sales pitches are coherent and aligned is an example of increasing sales by being able to communicate effectively.

Using the latest e-sales techniques is an example of boosting profits by having broad selling skills and knowledge.

Targeting products is an example of using knowledge of the customer and product to increase sales potential.

Introducing modern techniques is an example of how profits can be increased by having sales management and support skills.

Taking advantage of a competitor's weakness is an example of how being able to plan strategically can lead to an increase in sales.

Trends affecting sales

Professional selling is a discipline that's constantly changing. New theories and techniques are briefly heralded as the next great advancement in sales management. But all too often, they're quickly dismissed as obsolete, as newer trends emerge and require salespeople to adapt and update their skills and attitudes to remain competitive.

There are four main trends that affect the sales environment: constant advances in technology

the ever-increasing global marketplace the increasingly diverse workforce, and the rapid increase in competition

All sections of an organization, including sales, have to contend with technological advances – the first of the trends. Sophisticated technology that can help a sales team's performance is readily available.

Each team member should become skilled at using handheld devices, mobile computing, instant messaging, and all forms of social networking. These are a few ways technology has created new venues and channels for sales.

For example, a printer cartridge supply company begins receiving such a large number of orders through its web site that it creates a "click to talk live" function. This allows customers to interact in

Sales Foundation

real time with a customer service representative who has had sales training.

The second trend is concerned with the global marketplace. As globalization increases, companies feel pressure to seek sales penetration into foreign markets. Salespeople frequently spearhead this kind of initiative.

Salespeople need to grasp logistical demands, as well as try to establish relationships with customers from different cultural backgrounds. This process can be very slow.

Consider the example of a broadband solutions provider that has decided to move into a foreign market. The salespeople sent to the new market work hard, but progress is slow. Back at the company's head office, personnel in the Sales Department become frustrated at the lack of progress. Meanwhile the salespeople in the foreign market feel cut off and isolated, and their confidence is low.

Question

Match the trends that affect sales to the examples that represent them. Each trend may match to more than one example.

Options:

A. Technological advances

B. Global marketplace

Targets:

1. The Sales Department of an antique store increases sales by establishing a blog
2. A wine merchant's sales team becomes more time efficient by using instant messaging
3. A PC manufacturer's expansion into a foreign market is hindered by the language barrier
4. Sales begin poorly but gradually increase for a shoe company that enters a market in a different country

Answer

Establishing a blog is an example of the effect technological advances can have on sales.

Using instant messaging is an example of the effect of implementing technological advances in a sales environment.

A language barrier that slows progress is an example of the effect the global marketplace can have on sales.

A poor start followed by improvement is an example of what can happen to sales when entering the global marketplace.

The third trend that affects sales is the diverse workforce. For example, many Sales Departments now contain members of three or four different

Sales Foundation

generations.

Sales managers might face the problem that many of their experienced salespeople are nearing retirement, and there's not a sufficient supply of experienced workers to replace them.

Consider this example. A medium-sized window frame manufacturing company maintains a small sales force. The salespeople are all very experienced and consistently reach their targets. However, when some members of the team retire and new workers replace them, sales drop significantly.

The final trend in the sales environment is increased competition and the effect it has on sales. Because the sales environment is so competitive, salespeople need to have strategy-building capabilities.

Salespeople are becoming more focused on developing customer-centered relationships. These relationships are important to meeting revenue goals. This means that greater empowerment needs to be given to sales personnel.

For example, a metal fabrication company that faces encroachment into its territory gives its sales personnel increased permission to respond to requirement changes, opportunities, and any competitive threats that might emerge.

Sorin Dumitrascu

Question

Match the trends that affect sales to the examples that represent them. Each trend may match to more than one example.

Options:

A. Diverse workforce

B. Increased competition

Targets:

1. Lack of experience in a beverage company's sales team leads to a revenue slump

2. A sales manager for a textile company struggles to find professional sellers with adequate knowledge of the industry

3. An insurance sales manager encourages his team to think strategically in a cluttered marketplace

4. To survive in a crowded industry, a software seller adopts long-range planning techniques

Answer

A revenue slump occurring because a sales team lacks experience is an example of the effect the diverse workforce trend has on sales.

Struggling to find qualified salespeople is an example of the effect the diverse workforce trend can have on sales.

Promoting strategic thinking is an example of how the increased competition trend can affect sales.

Sales Foundation

Engaging in long-range planning is an example of the effect of the increased competition trend on sales.

Changes in the buyer-seller relationship

The buyer-seller relationship is finely balanced and subject to constant change. This is because buyers have become more knowledgeable, and their expectations have grown as a result. They expect salespeople to be as well informed as they are about products. There are four different ways that the buyer-seller relationship has changed as a result of the sales trends: increased seller cooperation, emphasis on relationship selling, focus on seller responsiveness, and enhanced scope for productivity.

The first change, increased seller cooperation, occurred as a result of the pressure on salespeople to satisfy both the needs of their own organizations as well as customers' organizations.

Salespeople are expected to accept the responsibility for delivering a successful outcome for both parties. Buying organizations increasingly expect selling organizations to work with them to find business solutions.

The second change in the buyer-seller relationship is the emphasis that has been placed on relationship selling. This means that salespeople have started to move away from transactional selling where the emphasis is on just selling a product. Instead, salespeople are engaging in consultative selling. This is where they assume the role of advisors to their customers. To achieve this, they put greater effort into establishing and maintaining deep relationships with customers.

The third change is the focus on seller responsiveness. This has resulted in sales professionals accepting that they might not be able to group their sales into specific monthly or quarterly results.

Sellers have had to adapt to the buyer's time frame. This requires them to remain focused on delivering on the agreed-upon terms of the sales contract. Often this can lead to tension in the selling organization, as it needs to show that revenue is being generated.

The temptation in the past was to try to push or coerce the buyer into making payment in a way that suited the selling organization. But this is no longer an option. Salespeople have to carry out a difficult balancing act of dealing with revenue demands, ethical and legal implications, and customer satisfaction.

The final change in the buyer-seller relationship is the enhanced scope for productivity. As the sales environment has changed, the traditional emphasis placed on quotas has decreased. Companies are now more interested in analyzing the profitability of specific sales to their customers. Selling organizations are implementing productivity measures that favor low-cost selling rather than direct selling. Also, employers increasingly demand more efficient time management of salespeople.

Question

Which examples represent the effects sales trends have had on the buyer-seller relationship?

Options:

1. A machinery salesperson struggles to satisfy the demands of both the buying and selling organizations

2. A sales manager with a sporting goods company views himself as an advisor to customers

3. The sales team of a semiconductor company organizes its reports around the buyer's payment schedule

4. The sales force for a textile manufacturer is given time management training

5. The sales manager at a plastics manufacturer insists that the sales team concentrate on transactional selling

6. A brewing company's sales manager expects customers to pay at times outlined by him

Answer

Sales Foundation

Option 1: This option is correct. When salespeople work to please their own organizations as well as buying organizations, it's an example of increased seller cooperation.

Option 2: This option is correct. Becoming an advisor to customers is an example of the emphasis placed on relationship selling.

Option 3: This option is correct. Reacting to the buyer's needs is an example of focusing on seller responsiveness.

Option 4: This option is correct. Trying to achieve time management efficiencies is an example of the enhanced scope for productivity.

Option 5: This option is incorrect. Transactional selling is being replaced by consultative selling as a result of the trends affecting sales.

Option 6: This option is incorrect. The recent trends affecting sales have seen selling organizations become more attuned to the specific needs of buying organizations.

Buyer Behavior

Understanding consumer buying behavior is the key to successful sales. There are several factors that can influence a buyer's decision to make a purchase. These include cultural, social, personal, and psychological factors. An effective salesperson should also know about the two types of demand that play a part in each buying decision process – primary demand and selective demand.

There are five stages of the buying decision process: recognition of need, search for information, evaluation of purchase options, decision to buy, and post-purchase evaluation. Sales professionals use this model of consumer behavior to learn what makes consumers buy products and services.

There are key differences between consumer and organizational buying. The first difference is that final customers generate organizational demand. The second is that organizations use goods for production or resale. The third difference is that consumers almost always purchase goods for personal consumption.

Consumer buying behavior

In all professions, there are some people who are good at their jobs and others who aren't. In sales, it's easy to tell the two apart. Good salespeople are patient, understanding, and knowledgeable about the products they're selling. They take a genuine interest in the needs of the buyer and will try to provide solutions to satisfy the buyer's needs.

Ineffective salespeople chase quick sales and use hard-selling tactics. This may result in a one-off sale, but customers will quickly become impatient with such behavior. A salesperson who is only interested in short-term personal gain can damage an organization's reputation by pressuring valued customers into making purchases they're not entirely happy with.

Sometimes a salesperson can misread a situation and put the buyer off by coming across as being too pushy. Another mistake inexperienced and ineffective sales professionals often make is believing that they know more than the customer.

Consider this example of a salesperson misreading a situation. Peter is a salesman working in a cell phone store. A teenage boy and his mother enter the store and ask to purchase a particular version of a cell phone. Peter explains that there is a newer version of that cell phone available and Peter assumes the teenager will want to purchase it.

However, the version of the cell phone the teenager wants has a particular type of camera the newer version doesn't. Both the teenager and his mother are annoyed that Peter is insisting on demonstrating the newer version.

All good salespeople will testify that understanding consumer buying behavior is the key to successful sales. Knowing what influences buying decisions can help avoid misunderstandings. There are several factors that can influence a buyer's decision to make a purchase. These include cultural, social, personal, and psychological factors.

Cultural

Cultural factors are those that have been instilled since birth. These include attitudes and beliefs, which influence how individuals make purchasing decisions. For example, if a person's parents had emigrated from another country, that person might be more likely to purchase food that originated from that country.

Social

Personal factors can include an individual's preference or taste for certain items. If a consumer likes the way a band sounds, that person is likely to purchase that band's albums.

Personal

Social factors also impact consumer buying behavior. For example, if the majority of the members of a person's peer group don't drink alcohol, that person is less likely to drink alcohol.

Psychological

Psychological factors also influence how a buyer makes a decision. These factors can depend on each individual's character. If someone is very outgoing and extroverted, it's likely that the person will spend money on entertainment and socializing. An introverted person is less likely to go out as often, and might make the majority of purchases online or through mail order.

In addition to understanding the factors that influence buyer behavior, a good salesperson should also know about the two types of demand that play a part in each buying decision process. Primary and selective demand are very different from each other, and each requires a unique approach from the salesperson.

Primary demand is when a prospective buyer expresses an interest in a product for the first time.

Buyers with a primary demand are at the stage where they're only considering the product, meaning it's unlikely that they've shopped around or made product comparisons.

It's up to the salesperson to convince the buyer that the product is the correct one before the buyer even contemplates another company's product. Primary demand situations provide a solid opportunity to gain new business.

Selective demand is when buyers discover they have a need for a particular product and go looking for it. Buyers with a selective demand will often approach the selling organization directly.

Buyers with a selective demand are harder to sell to. This is because they've had the opportunity to research what type of product they need.

The consumer will compare price, quality, and value with offers from other selling organizations.

Once a salesperson understands the consumer's decision-making process in relation to buying, there's an excellent chance of making the sale.

Being aware of the factors that influence the buyer's decisions, and the types of demand that prompt the buyer to seek solutions, can give a salesperson a competitive edge over others.

The seller will then be able to determine how to best serve the prospective buyer's needs. And the seller will know when it's appropriate to educate the buyer about the product.

Sales Foundation

Consider this example of how understanding consumer buying behavior can benefit a seller. Anne, a salesperson working for a computer retail store, greets a customer. The customer explains to Anne that he is interested in purchasing a computer for the first time.

Anne realizes that the customer's demand is in the primary category. This helps her as she makes the sale to the customer. She knows that the customer needs a computer that is user friendly and requires minimum hassle to set up.

Anne selects a product with these features in order to serve the buyer's need. Then she begins to educate the customer about computers in general and how the product she picked would be suitable for him. The customer buys the computer.

Question

What are the benefits of being able to understand consumer buying behavior?

Options:

1. A salesperson can decide how best to serve the potential buyer's needs

2. The salesperson will know when it's appropriate to educate the consumer about a product

3. A salesperson will be able to make a quick sale

4. The salesperson will be able to sell the consumer any product

Answer

Option 1: This option is correct. Using an approach aimed at meeting needs is more likely to result in a successful sale.

Option 2: This option is correct. Educating the customer at the wrong time could cause offense and potentially result in the loss of a sale.

Option 3: This option is incorrect. Focusing on making a quick sale could potentially harm the selling organization's reputation and significantly reduce the possibility of repeat business.

Option 4: This option is incorrect. The purpose of gaining an understanding of consumer buying behavior is that the right product can be sold to the customer. This ensures customer satisfaction and increases the potential for repeat sales.

The buying decision process

Sales professionals use various models of consumer behavior to learn what makes consumers buy products and services. This topic uses the buying decision process as a model. Each step in the process is subject to the influence of internal and external factors that ultimately impact the buying decision.

There are five stages in the buying decision process: 1. recognition of need

2. search for information

3. evaluation of purchase options 4. decision to buy, and

5. post-purchase evaluation

Consider this example, which explains the five stages of the buying decision process. A vinyl record collector has an extensive collection of rare vinyl records. He has had the same turntable for the past 15 years. It suddenly stops working, and he realizes that he'll need to purchase a new one if he wants to listen to his records. This realization forms the first stage of the buying decision process – he recognized a new need.

In the second stage of the buying decision process, searching for information, the collector decides to purchase a new turntable. However, vinyl is no longer as popular as it once was, and many stores only sell digital music players. He has to find a store that sells what he needs.

He locates a store in his area that sells turntables. The salesman shows him two different models. One is a basic model. The other is more expensive, but has a USB connection which will allow the collector to transfer his music to a computer hard drive.

This is the third step of the buying decision process, in which he recognizes a new need and evaluates the purchase options. He weighs the positive and negative aspects of each option.

After evaluating his options, the collector decides to purchase the basic turntable. This completes the fourth stage of the process, the decision to buy.

The collector takes the turntable home. But after a week, he begins to have doubts and regrets about not buying the model with the USB connection. He decides to return to the store to exchange the turntable.

By reviewing his purchase decision, the collector has completed the final stage of the process, the post- purchase evaluation.

Question

Lisa is an office manager for an insurance

Sales Foundation

company.

Sequence the stages of the buying decision process that Lisa goes through.

Options:

A. Lisa realizes her printer has stopped working

B. She browses through office supply catalogues to see what printers are available

C. She finds two printers that are suitable, but one is made by a well-established brand and the other isn't

D. She decides to purchase the printer from the well-known manufacturer

E. After the printer is installed, she decides that she made the correct decision

Answer

Lisa realizes her printer has stopped working is ranked the first stage in the process. By determining this new requirement, Lisa completes the first stage of the process, recognition of need.

She browses through office supply catalogues to see what printers are available is ranked the second stage in the process. By carrying out research about what printers are available, Lisa goes through the second stage of the process, search for information.

She finds two printers that are suitable, but one is made by a well-established brand and the other isn't is ranked the third stage in the process. By comparing different printers, Lisa completes the third stage of the process, evaluation of purchase options.

She decides to purchase the printer from the well-known manufacturer is ranked the fourth stage in the process. When she makes her decision to purchase the printer, Lisa completes the fourth stage of the process, decision to buy.

After the printer is installed, she decides that she made the correct decision is ranked the fifth stage in the process. By reviewing the situation after completing the purchase, Lisa completes the fifth and final stage of the process, post-purchase evaluation.

Consumer and organizational buying

In addition to examining the buying decision process, salespeople must consider the actual buyers themselves. There are two categories of buyer, consumer and organizational. Consumers are often referred to as the final customer by sales professionals, and their purchases are for personal, family, or household use. Organizational buyers include producers, resellers, governments, and institutions.

There are key differences between consumer and organizational buying. The first difference is that consumers, or final customers, generate organizational demand.

The second difference between the two markets is that organizations use goods for production or resale.

The third difference is that consumers almost always purchase goods for personal consumption.

There are differences between organizational and consumer transactions as well. Unlike consumers, organizations will often retain the services of a buying specialist to handle purchasing requirements. For example, a car manufacturer might outsource the purchasing of leather for seats to a person who specializes in purchasing leather only. Organizational transactions can also often involve dealing with more than one manager or department head. And, organizations set exact specifications when purchasing and will generally not tolerate any variances.

Question

Which examples represent the differences between organizational and consumer buying?

Options:

1. Consumer demand for cell phones in turn creates organizational demand for cell phone producers
2. A furniture company purchases large quantities of varnish for use on its products
3. A family purchases food for its own consumption
4. A food processing company creates consumer demand by purchasing large amounts of ingredients
5. A young woman spends the majority of her disposable income on finished goods she never uses

Answer

Option 1: This option is correct. Final customers generating organizational demand, in this case for cell phone producers, is one way that organizational and consumer buying differ.

Option 2: This option is correct. Organizations

Sales Foundation

use goods for production or resale. The furniture company uses the varnish as part of its production process.

Option 3: This option is correct. Consumers nearly always purchase finished goods for personal consumption.

Option 4: This option is incorrect. Organizational demand does not create consumer demand. However, consumer demand can lead to organizational demand.

Option 5: This option is incorrect. In most instances, consumers purchase finished goods for personal consumption.

An Introduction to the Sales Process

The sales process is a series of events that the seller will go through with a customer to begin and close a sales transaction. The sales process applies no matter what product or service is being sold, and is an essential part of any proper sales procedure.

Sales processes can vary in length, depending on the type of product being sold. This topic covers a five-stage sales process. The stages are finding potential buyers, qualifying, presentation, closing the sale, and asking for referrals.

The sales process

When a salesperson engages a customer and begins selling a product or service, it's the beginning of the sales process. This is a series of events that the seller will go through with a customer. Sales professionals use the sales process to begin a transaction, and hope to close the process successfully by making the sale.

The sales process is subject to variation. It can be a long process or a short one, depending on the type of product, how much it costs, and who the potential customer is.

Though there are different versions of the process, several common elements remain the same. The approach covered in this topic has five stages:

1. finding potential buyers,
2. qualifying,
3. presentation,
4. closing the sale, and
5. asking for referrals.

Following an effective sales process is essential for sales professionals to be successful. If the requirements for each stage of the process are handled properly, it can reduce the number of barriers, known as objections, that can block a sale. Objections can arise because the salesperson is selling the product to the wrong market, not asking the right questions, or making presentations that aren't geared toward customers' needs.

Question

Why do professional salespeople use the sales process?

Options:

1. To successfully initiate and close a sales transaction

2. To successfully manage the administrative functions associated with a sales transaction

3. To successfully incorporate the selling company's corporate message into sales strategies

Answer

Option 1: This is the correct option. By completing each stage of the sales process, a salesperson can increase the chance of successfully initiating and closing a sales transaction.

Option 2: This option is incorrect. The sales process is not specifically designed to help oversee or manage the administrative functions associated with a sales transaction. The process is intended to provide a pathway to a sale.

Option 3: This option is incorrect. While incorporating the selling company's corporate message into sales strategies can be important, it's

Sales Foundation

not the function of the sales process to carry this out.

Finding potential buyers and qualifying

The first stage of the sales process is finding potential buyers. This is also called prospecting. By taking the proper approach to this stage, sales professionals can save time and achieve greater market penetration.

Inexperienced salespeople sometimes make the mistake of pursuing an overly wide customer base.

It's much more efficient to have a focused strategy that targets suitable customers, rather than taking a scattershot approach.

A selling organization creates a profile of its ideal target customer based on the type of industry, the product, and the purchasing budget. Once this is complete, its sales personnel can then begin to prospect for potential buyers.

The key to finding new buyers is to look in the right places. For instance, if a telemarketer is selling snow chains for tires, there's no point calling customers who live in areas with warm climates.

There are many ways to prospect for new buyers: searching the Internet, checking the phone book, buying leads lists, and getting referrals, to name just a few.

Consider this example of a company that produces industrial lubricant for machinery and how

Sales Foundation

they find potential buyers. The company's sales department subscribes to various trade journals and magazines relating to manufacturing. The salespeople then use these publications to identify customers who might be interested in their product. These publications often carry profiles of individuals such as supply chain managers and procurement managers from specific companies. This helps salespeople to build their leads lists.

Question

Which example represents the first stage in the sales process, finding potential buyers?

Options:

1. A carpet seller attends an interior design convention to establish contacts

2. A salesperson for a rug company collaborates with the Marketing Department on a promotional strategy

3. An auto parts sales professional discovers that a company doesn't have the budget to support a purchase

Answer

Option 1: This is the correct option. Establishing contacts through networking is something that takes place in the finding potential buyers stage of the sales process.

Option 2: This option is incorrect. Collaborating with the Marketing Department on a promotional strategy is not an activity that takes place during the sales process. The sales process represents the selling process, rather than the promotion process.

Option 3: This option is incorrect. Discovering whether a company can afford a product is an activity that occurs during the second stage of the sales process, qualifying.

Qualifying is the second stage of the sales process. This is the point where salespeople make sure that the targeted buyer actually has a need for the product and can afford it.

Establishing this criteria early in the process can save a salesperson time. It's often the case that the buyer doesn't need the product or can't afford it – or sometimes both.

It's up to the individual seller to discover this information by carrying out research and asking the right questions.

These qualifying questions should be designed to extract as much useful information as possible from the prospective buyer.

After asking these questions of the buyer, the seller should know if the buyer has the authority to make the decision, whether the company wants the product, and whether the company can afford the product.

Matching the right product to the right customer is a crucial function of the qualifying stage.

Consider an example representing the qualifying stage. A software salesman compiles a list of questions to ask potential buyers. The questions are specifically designed to politely elicit responses that will let the seller know if the potential buyer is a decision-maker, and whether the company has the need and funding to support the sale.

Presentation, closing, and referrals

The third stage of the sales process is presentation. This is when the seller tells the prospective buyer about the product's merits.

To achieve success at this stage, a seller needs to know the product and the customer. The more information a seller has on each, the better the presentation will be.

The presentation stage can range from informal sales calls to very formal sales presentations made before representatives of the buying organization.

Salespeople can study and practice presentation skills. The presentation itself needs to be informative and demonstrative of the skill and intelligence of the seller.

Above all, the presentation needs to convey the seller's passion for the product.

When giving a presentation, a salesperson should be enthusiastic, brief, and sincere.

Here's an example featuring a saleswoman preparing for a presentation. The company she works for produces exercise equipment. She arranges to borrow one of the workout machines she is selling, and familiarizes herself with all aspects of the machine. She then visits many of the gyms owned by the potential buyers to see if they have a

Sales Foundation

similar machine. During the presentation, she demonstrates the machine and impresses the buyers with her knowledge of their industry.

Question

Match the stages in the sales process to the examples representing them.

Options:

A. Finding potential buyers
B. Qualifying
C. Presentation

Targets:

1. A printer salesperson buys a leads list
2. A salesperson realizes that the potential buyer can't authorize a purchase
3. A seller working for a property consultancy firm practices a sales pitch in front of colleagues

Answer

Buying a leads list is an example of an activity that occurs during the first stage of the sales process, finding potential buyers.

Realizing the person isn't a decision-maker is an example of an activity that occurs during the second stage of the sales process, qualifying.

Practicing a sales pitch is an example of an activity that happens in the third stage of the sales process, presentation.

Sorin Dumitrascu

Closing the sale is the fourth stage of the sales process. This is when the sale is finalized and the contract is signed.

Every aspect of sales leads toward this point. Closing the sale is the goal, and the other stages of the sales cycle are designed to help achieve this outcome.

There are hundreds of closing techniques, although none of them have been proven to be 100% effective. Different circumstances require different approaches to closing a deal.

To close any sales deal, the seller needs to establish a rapport with the buyer. Once this is achieved, the seller can begin to build a working relationship. Then the salesperson must analyze the buyer's organization or company to identify a problem or need to be solved or satisfied. The final aspect of closing is the most difficult for sales professionals, but also the most important – actually asking for the order.

Consider this example of how to close a sale. An insurance saleswoman is trying to sell a workplace insurance policy to a large retail company. She begins by establishing her credentials as an expert in insurance coverage.

Her honest and enthusiastic approach gains the

Sales Foundation

trust of the purchasing manager. The manager is impressed with the salesperson's determination to tailor an insurance policy to meet the retailer's needs.

The seller makes a final presentation to the purchasing manager, and then asks whether or not the manager wants to finalize the sale.

The final stage in the sales process involves asking for referrals. This occurs after a sale has been made, and when the buyer is satisfied with the product and how it was sold. The salesperson can ask the buyer to refer others to the selling organization. This process can generate excellent prospective buyers. The salesperson can ask the buyer for positive testimony that can be featured on the seller's web site or in promotional material.

Consider an example of a seller asking for referrals. John is a stationery supply salesperson. He secures a sales contract to supply a large government organization with all its stationery needs.

John receives positive feedback from the organization's purchasing manager who was very happy with all aspects of John's work on the sale.

John then asks the purchasing manager to refer any other organizations that the purchasing manager might have contact with to him.

Question

Match each stage in the sales process to the example of an activity that occurs during that stage.

Options:

A. Finding potential buyers
B. Qualifying
C. Presentation
D. Closing the sale
E. Asking for referrals

Targets:

1. A telemarketer selling mortgages uses the phone book to identify prospective clients
2. A sales representative for a diamond wholesaler uses a sales call to gauge a buyer's budget
3. A salesman times how long it takes to pitch his stain removal product
4. After finishing a test drive, a car salesman asks his customer if he wants to finalize the deal
5. After a sale, the telecommunications company asks the buyer to provide a positive testimonial

Answer

Using the phone book to identify prospective clients is an example of an activity that happens during the finding potential buyers stage of the sales process.

Sales Foundation

Finding out if a buyer is able to afford the product is an example of an activity that occurs during the qualifying stage of the sales process.

Practicing and timing a sales pitch is an example of an activity that can occur during the presentation stage of the sales process.

Asking if a customer wants to finalize the deal is an event that happens during the closing stage of the sales process.

Asking the buyer to provide a positive testimonial after a sale has been completed is something that can occur during the referral stage of the sales process.

CHAPTER 2 - Strategic Sales Planning

Analyzing the Competition and Segmenting Customers

Creating Value Propositions

Developing Your Sales Process

Practice: Developing a Sales Strategy

Analyzing the Competition and Segmenting Customers

The key steps of competitor analysis are to identify the competitors, research them, identify strengths and weaknesses, and determine your company's position in the marketplace.

Identifying market segments allows you to tailor sales efforts to customer needs. To be effective, segments must meet the criteria of being measurable, sustainable, accessible, diverse, and feasible.

Analyzing the competition

Maybe your company has a great product and loyal customers. But if you try to sell to the wrong group of customers, or if you use the wrong sales method, your product will never reach a wider audience. You need a sales strategy for true success. Sales strategies are plans that identify your customers and prospects, and the right ways to reach them.

A good sales strategy can help you identify the best opportunities and how to take advantage of them. You need to know who your market is and how to reach them.

Then you can achieve sales targets and increase profits, because your strategies for promoting and positioning your product or service will be more effective.

There are many benefits to a successful sales strategy:
- - it tailors the sales process to each target market's needs,
- it helps clarify sales objectives and increase sales relative to the competition,
- it monitors sales activities so you can make improvements,
- it helps focus attention on attractive market

Sales Foundation

segments that will appreciate your offering, and
- it helps shift selling emphasis away from price and toward value.

Before developing a sales strategy, you have to know exactly what your business is and how customers benefit from your products or services. You need to know who your ideal customer is, and how your company and products differ from the competition. A sales strategy has to be able to change when needed, to accommodate things such as transformations in customer needs, market shifts, or the economy.

Various processes and methods are used in competitor analysis, but there are four key steps:

1. identify your competition, which includes all businesses that address the same customer needs as you do,

2. research the competition, learning everything you can about how they operate,

3. identify the strengths and weaknesses of your competitors, and

4. determine the position your company occupies in the marketplace.

Identifying competitors

Identifying all your business's competitors isn't as easy as just driving around to locate other companies. You probably already know who your main competition is, but you need to compile lists of everyone in your market. Internet searches and industry associations can be invaluable.

Be sure to identify new, as well as long-standing, competitors. Look for any businesses that cater to the same consumer needs as your company does.

For example, an advertising company might list other ad agencies, both small and large, since each type plays a different role with clients.

But freelance copywriters, in-house writers, journalists, and even fill-in-the-blank templates bought online can all be competitors to an advertising agency.

Identifying your competitors means examining all types of competition, especially your primary and direct competition. But you should also include secondary or indirect competition from other industries. And don't forget to list your potential competitors – companies that might move in to your direct market. Consider this situation. Serge is a sales manager at a start-up company that

Sales Foundation

manufactures electronic accessories for smartphones, such as mobile credit card readers. He's trying to identify all his company's competitors.

Primary

Serge's primary competitors are the market leaders that dominate the smartphone accessories market. Most of these companies are large electronics or computer firms that adapt their current offerings for the smartphone market.

Secondary

The secondary and indirect competitors in Serge's case are standard credit card reader companies and major banks.

Potential

The potential competitors in Serge's market are the manufacturers of the smartphones. While they don't currently have them, they may develop applications that don't require external accessories to act as credit card readers.

Question

Consider this scenario. You're a sales representative for a hospital supply company.

Match each category of competitor to the relevant example in this situation.

Sorin Dumitrascu

Options:

A. Primary
B. Secondary
C. Potential

Targets:

1. Other medical or hospital supply companies in your neighborhood or who service your area
2. Small home care-only supply stores and well stocked local pharmacies
3. A large veterinary supply company that's rumored to be expanding into your market

Answer

Primary or direct competitors target your exact market, and will include local companies and those who deliver to your region.

Indirect or secondary competitors are not in your primary industry. Stores focused on home care or consumer medical supply may also carry medical supplies and pharmaceuticals.

You need to prepare for the possible effect of potential competitors – such as the veterinary supply company – even if they're not a direct threat at this point in time.

Researching the competition

After identifying the competition, you have to learn everything you can about them. Researching your competitors should be an ongoing process. From collecting marketing materials, to visiting locations, to calling and asking questions, you should always be gathering information. You can even shop at your competitors' stores to experience their environment and customer service for yourself.

You need information about how companies position themselves, what products are offered, and what they promote as their key differentiators. Product literature and brochures can help you learn about pricing, product lines, and distribution models.

Another way to collect competitive data is to go to trade shows, and analyze your industry's trade publications. And don't forget to ask your customers about what types of products and services they prefer and are seeking.

A competitive profile can help you organize all your competitive intelligence information. The profile should list basic information such as company name and location, but can also include the company's strategies and reasons for success. The profile can note how the competition reacts to industry change. In addition, the profile can include information about financial solidity and liquidity, which can often be gleaned from investor statements.

Identifying strengths and weaknesses

After you've found out all you can about your competitors, it's time to identify their strengths and weaknesses. Analyze all the information you gathered and determine why customers buy from them. It might be price, customer service, reputation, or perceived value. Identify any advantages they have in terms of production management, marketing, or operations. Then identify vulnerabilities or weaknesses in these same areas.

You can use a table to analyze competitor strengths and weaknesses. For each company, columns can list the factors appropriate to your industry, such as price, value, if service is provided, location, reputation, convenience, and employees.

Once the table is laid out, rate your competitors according to each factor, including comments about the ratings. For example, strengths might include great customer service, and weaknesses might include overly aggressive salespeople.

If you color code the positives and negatives – perhaps by putting strengths in green and weaknesses in red – you'll be able to immediately tell each competitor's overall status.

Sorin Dumitrascu

Question

Remember the scenario where you're a sales representative for a hospital supply company?

Identify examples of strengths and weaknesses that might be found in your competitor analysis.

Options:

1. The quality of product offerings are similar to yours, but they offer some products your company does not

2. Neither your company nor theirs offers a line of home health care supplies

3. A hospice care supply company is an indirect competitor to your business

4. Your company is developing a product for an underserved consumer need

Answer

Option 1: This is a correct option. If your competitors offer more products, they have a stronger product line than your company, even if the overall quality is the same.

Option 2: This is a correct option. It's a weakness if the competition doesn't serve a valid area of the market. In this case, the competitor's weakness is shared by your company.

Option 3: This is an incorrect option. Identifying the competition is a different step in competitor analysis than determining strengths and weaknesses.

Option 4: This is an incorrect option. Identifying competitor strengths and weaknesses can help you highlight an underserved need of your market, giving you an opportunity to develop a stronger product in that area. But that's a benefit of the analysis, not a weakness of the competition.

Determining your position

Only after finding out all you can about your competition can you compare them to your own company and figure out your position. You can determine if there are any holes in their product offerings or niche markets they might be missing, and how your business fills in the gaps. Focus on what your business does differently, and what you bring to your target market.

You can create a table of your own company's strengths and weaknesses similar to the one you made for your competitors. When you rank your company using the same categories, you'll have a clear picture of how you fit into the marketplace.

But when you make up the table for your company, leave space to list opportunities and threats. Analyzing the tables will help you identify areas of improvement and what characteristics you can leverage to gain more customers.

Determining your position allows you to use your company's strengths and take advantage of competitors' weaknesses.

Question

Guy is a sales manager for a manufacturing company. As part of forming his sales strategy, he's

Sales Foundation

analyzing his company's competition. He lists the two main competitors and learns everything he can about them. Then he looks at their strong points, and where they don't do so well.

Which statements accurately describe Guy's performance related to each of the steps in analyzing the competition?

Options:

1. He identifies his primary, secondary, and potential competitors

2. He investigates his primary competition

3. He identifies his primary competition's strengths and weaknesses

4. He determines his company's position relative to his competitors

5. He identifies his primary competitors, but not his secondary or potential competitors

6. He identifies all his competitors' strengths and weaknesses

Answer

Option 1: This is an incorrect option. Guy should list all the businesses that address the same customer needs.

Option 2: This is a correct option. By learning everything he can, Guy carries out the second step of competition analysis.

Option 3: This is a correct option. When Guy

looks at strong and weak points, he's carrying out the third step in analyzing the competition.

Option 4: This is an incorrect option. Guy stops his analysis after the third step. He doesn't determine the position his company has in the marketplace.

Option 5: This is a correct option. Guy should have listed all the businesses that address the same customer needs, not just the primary ones.

Option 6: This is an incorrect option. Guy only identifies his primary competition's strengths and weaknesses. He should have done the same for secondary and potential competitors.

Segmenting customers

Once you've analyzed your competition, you can begin to think about another vital part of your business – your customers. Most companies have many possible customers – too many, in fact, to be able to cater to each individual need, preference, and behavior. So the second step in creating your sales strategy is to segment customers and prospective customers. Segmentation is the process of identifying groups of buyers who have similar purchasing desires, characteristics, and price sensitivities.

Market segmentation organizes customers and prospects into groups that value similar products or services, and respond in predictable ways to marketing or promotional offers.

When you segment a market, you can focus on the subset of prospects that is most likely to purchase your offering. The common characteristics of the segment allow you to develop one marketing mix for all the customers in the group.

And customers are generally willing to pay a premium for a product that best meets their specific needs. If done properly, segmentation helps you to address customer wishes more effectively, build more sustainable customer relationships, and ensure the highest return for your marketing and sales expenditures.

The bases for segmentation are those characteristics that are consistent within groups but vary from one group to another. You can segment a consumer market using three primary bases:

- • geographic segmentation, which is based on regional factors such as climate and population density,
- customer segmentation, which is based on consumer demographic characteristics – the aspects of society or culture that are measurable, such as age and gender, and
- behavioral segmentation, which includes such variables as customer buying patterns and rates of product use.

Business markets are different in nature to consumer markets. Select each segmentation base for more information.

Geographic segmentation

Geographic segmentation in the business market tends to be based on regional variables such as the concentration of customers in an area, the specific regional industrial growth rate, and national and global economic factors.

Customer segmentation

Sales Foundation

Customer segmentation in the business market is based on variables such as the size of companies, what industry they're in, and their position in the value chain.

Behavioral segmentation

Behavioral segmentation in the industrial or business market has to do with buyer behavior such as loyalty to suppliers, usage patterns, and order size.

Whether for a business or consumer market, the basic process of segmentation involves creating segmentation criteria. You have to establish what customers need and which customers experience the need.

Then the market segment is determined by matching the benefits of your product or service with the customer needs.

For businesses, the need your product or service satisfies might fall into strategic, operational, or functional categories. Some businesses have to reduce expenses, such as downsizing companies. Others need to improve cash flow, productivity, or quality, such as businesses with complex manufacturing processes. Individual consumers also have functional needs – for a basic cell phone, for instance – but they may also have status or pleasure needs, such as for the latest or most expensive cell phone.

There are five criteria to help you determine if you've created an effective segment:

- it must be measurable, so you can determine the values of the factors used for segmentation,
- it should be sustainable, so it needs to be sufficiently large, with the profit potential to economically justify itself as a separate segment,
- it has to be accessible, so you must be able to reach the audience through existing communication and distribution methods,
- it must be diverse enough that it responds uniquely to the marketing mix, and
- it has to be feasible, allowing you to approach each segment with a particular marketing program that will bring you advantages.

Measurable

The differentiating variables must be measurable so you have a way to identify them. A company's own customer database can give information on buying behavior, such as frequency of purchase, volume, product identification, and methods of payment. Common measurable statistics also include age, income, and occupation.

Sustainable

To be sustainable, the segments should be durable so you don't need frequent changes to the sales plan. Statistics about frequency of usage and brand loyalty can help you decide if a segment is large enough to justify separate marketing activities. Demographic preferences – such as being urban or rural – can also help you determine sustainability.

Accessible

To be accessible, your company has to be able to reach the target segment and serve it. If you're going to advertise in target-group-specific media, such as magazines or web sites, you have to ensure your desired audience uses them.

Diverse

There's no use spending money on separate marketing campaigns if your target markets aren't diverse enough to justify them. For example, if both older, affluent consumers and younger, career-driven consumers respond the same way to convenience services, the segments are not diverse enough to warrant different marketing mixes.

Feasible

For segments to be feasible, the marketing has to

be practical. For instance, a small start-up company might not be able to afford to market to CEOs and top executives, even if it identifies them as a desired segment.

Question

Match the criteria for effective segmentation to their descriptions.

Options:

A. Measurable
B. Sustainable
C. Accessible
D. Diverse
E. Feasible

Targets:

1. Segmentation bases have definite specified values
2. Segments are large or have enough potential profit to be durable
3. Segments are reachable by current communication and distribution channels
4. Segments are composed of distinct elements, which are unalike
5. Segments can be approached with a particular marketing program that works

Answer

Measurable segments use values that can be

specified, such as age or zip code. Sustainable segments are large enough to justify separate marketing activities. Accessible segments are able to be served by the organization.

Diverse segments are distinct enough to respond differently to sales strategies. Feasible segments are those that are possible to market to easily and conveniently.

Segments commonly used for consumer and business markets include geographic, demographic, and behavioral bases. For instance, a market segment identified as "male business managers between 30 and 60 years old who earn more than $35,000 a year" includes the demographic bases of age, gender, and income. The segment "California drivers of hybrid cars" uses both geographic and behavioral bases for segmentation.

Once segmentation helps you determine who your best customers are likely to be, you need to target that group. After all, not all prospective customers know about your company or can tell the difference between you and your competition.

To target a particular segment, look for opportunities, such as customers with unmet needs, that are a good match for your products or services.

Keeping the criteria for segmentation in mind

will help you determine not just the potential profitability of a group, but also whether your company can meet the needs of those customers better than any of your competitors.

For example, consider Taku, a sales executive with a real estate development firm. Taku's company has a new condominium complex that features rooftop gardens for each three-bedroom unit.

One of Taku's market segments is "retired couples with incomes between $60,000 and $80,000" and another is "young, married couples with incomes between $60,000 and $80,000."

His current marketing channels already reach similar segments in a slightly lower income bracket.

Taku did well. His market segments of "young married couples with incomes between $60,000 and $80,000" and "retired couples with incomes between $60,000 and $80,000" are measurable, because they're based on demographic statistics of age and income.

The segments are sustainable, because they're large groups with needs that won't change constantly. They're accessible to Taku's real estate company through its regular sales channels.

The segments are diverse, because young

Sales Foundation

married couples and retirees react differently to marketing promotions. And they're feasible segments, because each is possible to approach.

Question

Now consider a different scenario. You're a salesperson at an electronics firm. You've heard from a colleague that there's a growing market for the use of Global Positioning System, or GPS, technology among children in case they get lost on the way home from school. You want to go after this segment for your GPS product. Because this is a new idea, you're not clear if you'd be selling to the children, to schools, or to parents, so you don't know what features you should highlight. You do know technological development in electronics changes rapidly.

Is the youth market an effective segment in this case, and why or why not?

Options:

1. No, because it's not measurable or diverse
2. No, because it's not sustainable
3. Yes, it's an effective segment that fits all criteria
4. No, because it's not accessible or feasible
5. Yes, because it's measurable

Answer

Option 1: This is an incorrect option. Age is a segmentation basis that can be measured, and there's sufficient diversity between the children and their parents or caretakers.

Option 2: This is a correct option. Sustainability is unlikely due to the rapid pace of technological development. GPS use for youth might be obsolete in a year and replaced with something new.

Option 3: This is an incorrect option. The segment doesn't meet all the criteria of being measurable, sustainable, accessible, diverse, and feasible.

Option 4: This is a correct option. The segment can't be accessed, nor is it feasible – with no clear idea of who you're marketing to, you can't approach them with a specific marketing program.

Option 5: This is an incorrect option. The segment is measurable and diverse, but it doesn't meet all the other criteria of being sustainable, accessible, and feasible.

Creating Value Propositions

A strong value proposition has many benefits. It defines what sets you apart from the crowd, it validates your business strategy, and it helps you price your products and services appropriately.

The three steps in creating a value proposition are to identify your customer, identify your customer's problems, and identify your company's unique solution.

Benefits of value propositions

If you had just 30 seconds in which to describe why people should buy your company's products or services, what would you say? Being able to answer this simple question means you know your value proposition. Value propositions are clear, concise statements explaining the results customers get if they buy or use your products or services. Compelling value propositions lie at the heart of sales, and creating them is the third step in developing a sales strategy.

You may know that your company has a great product or service that no one else can beat. But your customers and prospects won't be aware of that unless you can communicate it.

For example, if your product provides high value but your sales strategy can't describe it, you'll only convey vague messages about your products and services. If your value proposition says "we're the best" or "highly rated," customers might be left thinking "anyone can say that."

A strong value proposition tells your customers what your company will provide in exchange for their money. It's the promise you make to your customers.

Value propositions distill all the complexity of

what you provide into a phrase that's easy to remember, forming an integral part of sales strategies. While the main source of value for customers is of course your product itself, the value proposition can extend the worth of the product beyond its physical characteristics. It creates interest so sales prospects ask questions. It communicates to customers what's in it for them and why they should buy from you.

There are three main benefits to creating a strong and unique value proposition:
- it differentiates you from the competition,
- it validates your business strategy, and
- it helps you price your services appropriately.

Consider this strong value proposition for an engineering company: "We are the exclusive provider of patented software that reduces manufacturing waste by an average of 5% a year."

Differentiates you from the competition
Saying "exclusive provider" and "patented software" immediately proves that this company is different from its competitors.

Validates your business strategy
By being centered on customers' needs, a value

proposition can win you a greater market share. Including demonstrated results such as "5% a year" validates the company's business strategy of focusing on waste reduction.

Helps you price services

By clearly laying out the cost savings and that it is patented software, the value proposition reflects the benefits the software can bring to customers, and the expertise that was needed to create it. You can then price your services as a true reflection of all your work and time.

Question

Why are value propositions so important?

Options:

1. They define what sets you apart from the crowd
2. They validate the strategy your business is using
3. They help you price your services appropriately
4. They help validate your financial planning
5. They help mask any problems your product may have

Answer

Option 1: This is a correct option. A value proposition answers the question "Why should I buy from you and not from someone else?," so it differentiates your offer from your competitors' offers.

Option 2: This is a correct option. A value proposition has demonstrated results that help increase revenues, decrease costs, and improve operational efficiency, thus validating the business strategy.

Option 3: This is a correct option. Because a value proposition encompasses all you do to address customer needs, it helps you price your services to reflect the time and expertise that go into the work.

Option 4: This is an incorrect option. A value proposition can help validate your business and sales strategies, but it doesn't help in financial planning.

Option 5: This is an incorrect option. A value proposition can get a prospect to try a product, but the product itself still has to have tangible benefits.

Writing a value proposition

A good value proposition has to be clear, make sense, and address a problem customers have. You have to understand your customers' concerns before you can define what makes your product the best choice. It also allows you to connect with your customers in a way no other sales tool can. It can help you emphasize the services, programs, and processes that support products and assist customers.

A strong value proposition addresses three areas of customer benefits. Functional benefits include the physical aspects of the product or service; emotional benefits focus on the feelings created when buying or using the product; and self-expressive benefits contribute to your customers' views of themselves.

To fulfill the functional, emotional, and self-expressive needs of customers, a good value proposition should have four basic characteristics:
- • it should be motivating and useful to customers,
- it should communicate value to customers,
- it should address the information needed to be believable, and
- it should provide a solution for the customer.

Remember the value proposition for the

engineering company? "We are the exclusive provider of patented software that reduces manufacturing waste by an average of 5% a year."

Select each characteristic for information about how this value proposition addresses it.

Be motivating and useful
The functional benefit – such as reducing waste by 5% a year – is a unique element that customers care about, so it's motivating and useful.

Communicate value
The specifics of how much waste will be reduced is a clear statement of value.

Be believable
Because the value proposition discusses the exclusive patented software and gives specifics about the waste that will be reduced, it appears to be accurate and believable.

Provide a solution
For any manufacturing customer with a waste reduction need, this statement clearly provides the solution and indicates how much that solution will help.

Question
What are the characteristics of a good value proposition?

Options:

1. Motivates and proves useful to customers
2. Communicates value to customers
3. Gives the information needed to make it believable
4. Provides a solution for customers
5. Informs customers about the history of your organization
6. Communicates corporate goals to customers

Answer

Option 1: This is a correct option. A value proposition should drive customers to the point of purchase by convincing them that your product or service is the right one.

Option 2: This is a correct option. A value proposition should clearly let customers know why the product or service from your company is the best for their needs.

Option 3: This is a correct option. A value proposition should provide customers with enough information and specifics to allow them to evaluate it effectively.

Option 4: This is a correct option. A value proposition should clearly communicate the solution to customers' needs.

Option 5: This is an incorrect option. While the history of your organization may be of interest to some customers, it is not usually part of a value proposition.

Option 6: This is an incorrect option. A value proposition should communicate value to customers, not company goals.

Writing a strong value proposition can be an intimidating prospect. After all, it's vital to your sales strategy. To focus on the value your product or service provides to customers, follow three simple steps:

1. identify your customers – this becomes easier after you've analyzed your competition and segmented your customers in the first two stages of developing a sales strategy,

2. identify the problems or challenges that your customers have, and

3. identify the unique solution your product or service can bring to the customers' problem.

Identify your customers

For the first step, you need to understand who your target customers are so you can ensure your value proposition reflects an unfulfilled need. Be specific when identifying your target customers – for example, don't just identify "global companies," "seniors," or "men."

Identify your customers' problems

You need to analyze your customers' needs and challenges. If your product or service doesn't fulfill a need, it doesn't matter how unique it is. When you truly understand your customers, you can use your knowledge to improve their situations.

Identify your unique solution

Once you've identified the customers' problems, you look at the advantages your product can bring and how it's unique from the competition. Using metrics to identify the positives that result from your product or service shows customers its value. When it's clear your product can uniquely help them, customers recognize value and won't make pricing their only purchasing consideration.

Consider this example. Nancy, a sales executive for a web portal company, and her assistant, Juan, are creating a value proposition for their B2B – that is, business-to-business – customizable portal templates. The company's portals are much more than search engines, since they include access to data such as stock reports, news, and e-mail services.

Follow along as Nancy and Juan create a strong value proposition.

Sales Foundation

Nancy: First, we need to identify our customers.

Juan: Well, for this portal our target market is small businesses, right?

Nancy: Yes, but let's be more specific. We're looking for owners of small businesses that are not high-tech.

Juan: That's right. So now we need to identify the challenges facing our customers. They complain the most about how long it takes to set up portals, and that they end up not looking anything like the rest of their web site.

Nancy: Yes, and those are just the problems our templates solve. They're fully customizable while still being easy to use. None of our competitors can say that.

Juan: Great! So should our value proposition state "Our company has the best customizable web portals for small business owners?"

Nancy: That's a good start, but we need to back up our claims and be more specific. Let's use "Our customizable web portal templates for small businesses take 20% less time to build, and mirror your own site's look and feel. They're so easy to use, you don't have to be an IT expert."

Nancy and Juan's strong value proposition specifies who the product is designed for with "you don't have to be an IT expert," and it addresses the difficulty of customizing when it says "easy to use," and "mirror your own site's look and feel." It also provides the solution that nobody else has and tells how that's an advantage when it says "take 20% less time to build."

Consider how a training company might be able to turn a weak value proposition into a strong one. Follow along to review some examples.

Weak: Our training courses will increase your sales.

Strong: Our customized sales training courses increase prospect conversion ratios by an average of 20% in the first year.

Weak: We improve communication and morale.

Strong: Our team-building courses increase employee satisfaction and retention rates by a minimum of 10%.

A value proposition is the key to marketing and sales efforts. Research and test it to ensure it works, and truly differentiates your solution. It needs to have enough depth to permeate your marketing efforts, and the product or service must follow through. Customers expect what the value proposition promises. If your product doesn't benefit

Sales Foundation

them, the best value proposition in the world won't help.

Question

A sales executive is writing a value proposition for a headhunting firm. He decides his targets are multinational companies with diverse teams of workers. These companies have high rates of employee turnover, which leads to lower productivity. He creates a value proposition step by step that reads "Our firm helps you cut costs and increase employee retention in a global marketplace."

Which steps in writing a value proposition has the sales executive carried out correctly?

Options:

1. Identifying customers as multinational companies with diverse teams of workers

2. Identifying the customers' problems as high rates of employee turnover leading to lower productivity

3. Identifying the solution as cutting costs and increasing employee retention

4. Identifying his competitors in the global headhunting marketplace

Answer

Option 1: This is a correct option. The sales

executive correctly identified the customers for his target market.

Option 2: This is a correct option. The sales executive correctly analyzed his customers' needs by identifying the challenges they face.

Option 3: This is an incorrect option. The value proposition is not specific enough, and cutting costs is not a solution to the customers' need for better employee retention.

Option 4: This is an incorrect option. Identifying competitors is one of the ways to analyze the competition, not to write a value proposition.

Developing Your Sales Process

The benefits of having a sales process are that it helps you standardize customer interaction in sales, establish rapport with the client, sell more efficiently, generate more accurate sales and revenue reports, and estimate the revenue and ROI of your campaigns.

The basic steps in a sales process are prospecting, contacting, qualifying, presenting, discovering, closing the sale, and following up and providing service after the sale.

Benefits of a sales process

Once you've analyzed the competition, segmented the target market, and created a value proposition, you come to the fourth step in the development of a sales strategy. Now that you have a solid idea of the features and benefits of your product or service, it's time to develop your sales process. If you're going to deliver the right value proposition to the right customers, you need to know what sales activities to undertake, and when.

The sales process defines each step you take, from the initial lead to the final conversion of prospects to customers.

The connection you make with your customers is more effective when you have an organized and defined sales process for each market segment.

The value of having different sales processes

You may have noted that the sales process helps you add value by addressing customer needs. For example, one customer might know very little about your product. She might need a lot of product advice, training, and support. She may also need information about post-sale support services.

Another customer might be an expert who knows exactly what she wants. She won't need much advice or support, but she needs good pricing

Sales Foundation

and a highly efficient buying process. To be successful at selling to both customers, you need two different value propositions and sales processes.

The steps in any particular sales process will depend on many factors. These include customer needs, product features and characteristics, the industry, and the strategies and culture of both the company selling the product and the one purchasing it.

But it will always be a systematic and logical progression that can be reasonably expected to result in a sale.

There are many benefits to having a defined sales process:
- it helps you standardize customer interactions in sales, such as how much information is presented at each stage of the process,
- you can more easily establish rapport with customers, because your process will be based on their needs,
- it helps you sell more efficiently because you'll be able to understand and continually improve sales cycle metrics,
- you can generate more accurate sales and revenue reports because the process gives

everyone a common language to describe and measure sales productivity, and
- you'll be able to estimate the revenue and return on investment, or ROI, of your campaigns because you can predict how many leads become customers and what those leads are worth.

A newly hired sales manager, Kurt, is taking over an inefficient department that has been producing inaccurate sales reports. When Kurt puts a well-designed sales process in place, his department can finally measure the number of prospects, how long it takes to close sales, and how much revenue is generated. Because of the accuracy of the reports, team members now give the right amount of information to prospects, which helps them make decisions more quickly.

Question

What are the benefits of having a sales process?

Options:

1. Standardize your sales interactions with customers
2. Establish rapport with prospects and customers
3. Sell more efficiently overall
4. Generate more accurate sales and revenue

reports

    5. Estimate the revenue and return of campaigns

    6. Give you higher employee retention

    7. Reduce your sales staff

Answer

Option 1: This is a correct option. A sales process helps you standardize customer interactions at every stage, from the first lead to closing the sale.

Option 2: This is a correct option. A sales process allows you to establish rapport more easily because your focus is customer-centric.

Option 3: This is a correct option. A sales process helps you sell more efficiently because it generates a wealth of information about sales cycle metrics.

Option 4: This is a correct option. With a well-defined sales process, you can generate more accurate sales and revenue reports because the metrics are predictable and allow you to measure and track all aspects of the process.

Option 5: This is a correct option. A sales process helps you estimate the revenue and ROI of sales and marketing campaigns because you can measure and track effectiveness and conversion rates.

Option 6: This is an incorrect option. A sales process won't guarantee you'll have higher employee retention, although effective salespeople do generally have higher morale than ineffective ones.

Option 7: This is an incorrect option. A sales process won't guarantee that you can reduce your sales staff. Not all sales efficiencies result in staff reductions.

Steps in the sales process

You can think of selling as a process that flows logically from beginning to end in a series of predictable, easily identifiable steps. Each step builds on the previous one as the process moves from a first interaction to a closed sale. Sales processes will be slightly different for each situation, but most will include a few basic elements.

Each step has a measurable outcome that leads to the next activity, even though the particular steps involved in the process will depend on a variety of factors.

Because the outcomes can be assessed, you can use metrics to improve the skills of the salespeople and the sales process itself.

While each of the steps is found in one form or another in almost any sales process, there isn't one ultimate progression. The exact structure of a sales process is determined by the market sector and industry, the policies and procedures of the companies involved, and even government or trade restrictions, if applicable. A sales process may be finished in minutes or it may take months, depending on the product, service, or overall situation.

There are seven steps common to most sales processes which help you guide potential customers from initial contact to purchase:

1. prospecting, where you identify and connect with your prospective buyers,

2. contacting, where you research prospective buyers and initially approach them,

3. qualifying, where you sort through leads to determine which ones are worth pursuing,

4. presenting, where you match your offering with your potential customers' needs,

5. discovering, where you handle any problems or challenges your prospect has with your solution or prices,

6. closing the sale, which involves moving the conversation to the completion of the sale, and

7. following up and servicing after the sale.

Prospecting is typically the first step in the sales process. When you prospect, you identify potential customers, often by following up on leads. Since you can't make a sale without a customer, making sure there's a reasonable possibility someone will buy what you're offering is what turns a lead into a prospect.

In some companies, advertising generates leads that are then turned over to the sales department. In other cases, salespeople follow their own leads and

Sales Foundation

initiate a dialogue to find out if the person is truly interested in the product or service.

Of course, you can't prospect effectively without having a thorough knowledge of your products and services. You need to know what your ideal customer is like for each market segment. Only then can you apply prospecting techniques, such as cold calls and seminars.

Possible prospecting techniques

You may have noticed that the bulk of your prospects come to you by simply walking in, especially if you work in a store or business location. You may have prospects contact you by phone, mail, e-mail, or through your web site or social media pages. Anyone who requests information, asks any questions, or has made a previous purchase is also a potential prospect. Your customer relationship management, or CRM, software can be very useful in generating prospects.

The second step in the sales process is contacting, which is the initial approach phase. A good approach is crucial, because without it, a prospect may identify you as just another bothersome salesperson. But if you've done your homework, you can be viewed as an obliging person with something of value to offer. The only way to make this happen is to learn all you can before you approach your prospects.

Contacting prospects takes time and energy. Learning about them first allows you to determine your sales approach, and identify which products and services are best for a particular prospect. It can also reveal reasons why you shouldn't pursue some prospects, saving you time and resources.

Preparing this information beforehand gives you the details you need to understand the prospect's company and its position in its industry.

For example, if you read press releases from your prospect's company, you can make statements during the appointment such as "I understand your company is expanding into the wholesale market." The prospect will know you've done your research and are interested, which will likely build trust and respect.

The next step, qualifying, involves making sure the prospects are able to buy your product and are potentially willing. You need to concentrate on those prospects who are likely to give you a return on your investment of time, money, and energy. Qualification can take place through print or online methods, or in initial conversations with prospects. Asking questions allows you to learn more about the

Sales Foundation

prospect's business and relate that knowledge to your products, making them more attractive.

Asking open-ended, well thought-out questions will encourage prospects to talk so you can determine if they possess three essential things:

- A need for your service or product now or soon. For example, if you sell cars people normally keep for four years, a good prospect is an owner of a three-year-old car, not someone who bought a new one last year.
- A budget that's sufficient to buy your product or service. For instance, if a prospect truly can't afford to buy what you sell, you need to find out so you can move on.
- The authority to take action and make the purchase. For example, when a company has a simple and streamlined decision-making process, you have a better chance of closing a sale.

Question

What are the first three steps of the sales process?

Options:

1. Prospecting
2. Contacting
3. Qualifying

4. Presenting
5. Discovering
6. Closing the sale

Answer

Option 1: This is a correct option. Prospecting, or finding customers interested in your product or service, is the first step of the sales process.

Option 2: This is a correct option. Doing the research that allows you to make the initial contact is the second step of the sales process.

Option 3: This is a correct option. Ensuring prospects have the budget and authority to buy is qualifying, which is the third step of the sales process.

Option 4: This is an incorrect option. Presenting the sales demonstration is the fourth step of the sales process.

Option 5: This is an incorrect option. Discovering and answering any questions or objections related to the product or service is the fifth step of the sales process.

Option 6: This is an incorrect option. Closing the sale, when the purchase is officially made, is the sixth step of the sales process.

The fourth step in the sales process is the sales presentation. At this point in the process, you talk

Sales Foundation

about the features and functions of your products, and point out how they'll save the prospect money or time.

Keep your focus on the specific problem your product or service solves, and keep asking questions. Avoid making the presentation about yourself or your company. There should be a dialogue to determine if your company can best serve the prospect's company.

For example, instead of telling a prospect about the newest and most expensive item in your product line, keep the focus of the discussion on the one product or service that has the most benefit.

In the fifth step, discovering, you handle your prospect's concerns. This step is where prospects may challenge your solutions or your pricing. For example, you may be asked many questions or hear objections about your offering, but that's a good thing. You need to discover what information your prospect needs to make a decision. Objections are clues that the customer doesn't completely understand. Listen carefully and respond by explaining thoroughly and by adding a benefit.

After you make your sales presentation and answer your prospect's questions and objections, you need to close the sale. Closing isn't a slick technique. It's the culmination of a good sales process.

Closing is simply the completion of the sale, when a prospect turns into a customer. The key to closing is your ability to move the conversation to a logical conclusion, asking the buyer to commit.

There are several actions you can take to close a sale:

- Closing on specific actions involves deciding on the action to be taken and identifying those responsible for the action.
- Developing a timetable involves documenting the action plan and gaining agreement on specific steps, individual assignments, criteria for success, and dates for completion.
- Being assumptive means being positive. It involves making statements that assume agreement from your customer. However, that doesn't mean that you don't verify these assumptions with the customer.

The sales process doesn't end with the placement of the first order. After the closing, you still need to follow up and provide service. Good follow up can help you increase your closing ratio because it nurtures the relationship you've built with your customer. When you follow up, you can gauge a prospect's continued willingness to buy, or to

Sales Foundation

discuss other solutions. To follow up well, keep detailed notes on each customer, preferably in a central database.

Question

The final step of the sales process is following up after the sale.

Sequence examples of the first six steps in the sales process.

Options:

A. A person responds to an ad and wants information

B. A salesperson researches a prospect before calling

C. A salesperson calls to discuss a prospect's needs and budget

D. A salesperson demonstrates product features and benefits

E. A salesperson responds to all a prospect's objections

F. The prospect signs a contract and makes a payment

Answer

A person responds to an ad and wants information is ranked the first step. People contacting you for information is an example of prospecting, the first step in the sales process.

Sorin Dumitrascu

A salesperson researches a prospect before calling is ranked the second step. Researching a prospect is an example of contacting, the second step in the sales process.

A salesperson calls to discuss a prospect's needs and budget is ranked the third step. Calling a prospect to discuss needs and budget is qualifying, the third step in the sales process.

A salesperson demonstrates product features and benefits is ranked the fourth step. Explaining features and benefits is an example of presenting, the fourth step in the sales process.

A salesperson responds to all a prospect's objections is ranked the fifth step. Responding to objections is an example of discovering, the fifth step in the sales process.

The prospect signs a contract and makes a payment is ranked the sixth step. Signing a sales agreement is an example of closing, the sixth step in the sales process.

Practice: Developing a Sales Strategy

A sales strategy gives your business consistency. It allows your sales team to know who its customers and prospects are, what its objectives are, and what the competition is doing. The metrics that result from having a strategy and standardized sales processes will help your understanding and forecast, and improve your sales.

Developing a sales strategy consists of analyzing the competition, segmenting customers, creating value propositions, and crafting a sales process.

Creating a sales strategy

Does this situation sound familiar? Aiko is a sales representative with a busy manufacturing company. All too often, she gives people information about a product, then never hears from them again. She doesn't know why some prospects end up buying and others don't. This means she also never knows how many real prospects are in the pipeline or what they might be worth to the company. Her sales process doesn't seem to match how her prospects want to buy.

Aiko is a talented salesperson, but she needs to develop an overall sales strategy. Sales strategies are plans that include analyzing your competitors and identifying customers and prospects. They involve segmenting your target markets and determining their needs and desires so you can create strong value propositions. They also help you develop a sales process that allows you to reach customers and sell your product or service.

Analyzing the competition

Competitor analysis involves identifying your competitors and evaluating their strategies.

The key steps to analyzing your competition are to identify primary, secondary, and potential competitors, find out everything you can about them, and identify their strengths and weaknesses. Then you'll be able to determine your own company's position in your marketplace.

Segmenting customers

You have to be able to identify market segments – groups of prospective buyers that have common needs and desires – so you can tailor your sales efforts accordingly.

Market segments have to meet the criteria of being measurable, sustainable, accessible, diverse, and feasible.

Creating value propositions

Value propositions allow your customers to answer the questions "What's in it for me?" and "Why should I buy from you?"

The steps in creating value propositions are to determine who your customers are, identify their needs and problems, and be able to clearly specify what your company's unique solution is.

Developing a sales process

A sales process is a standardized and systematic approach to selling your product or service.

There are seven steps in most sales processes: prospecting, contacting, qualifying, presenting, discovering, closing the sale, and finally, providing service and follow up after the sale.

If Aiko had a sales strategy, she would be able to measure and improve her sales performance and productivity. A step-by-step plan would bring her closer to her goals and allow her to understand the results she gets. She would better understand her customers' needs. And greater understanding helps to build confidence and would allow Aiko to feel she's in control.

Case Study: Question 1 of 3
Scenario

For your convenience, the case study is repeated with each question.

A sales team at a pharmaceutical company is gearing up for the launch of a new medication. The company markets and sells to doctors and hospitals worldwide.

Answer the questions in order.

Question

Which of the main steps in the development of the sales strategy was overlooked?

Options:

1. Analyzing the competition
2. Segmenting customers
3. Creating value propositions
4. Developing a sales process

Sales Foundation

Answer

Option 1: This is an incorrect option. The sales team gathered information and analyzed the competition in this scenario.

Option 2: This is the correct option. Sales team members did not segment their customers and prospects.

Option 3: This is an incorrect option. The sales team created a value proposition in this scenario.

Option 4: This is an incorrect option. The team developed a valid sales process for its product.

Case Study: Question 2 of 3

Which of the steps that were performed in the development of this sales strategy need more work?

Options:

1. Analyzing the competition
2. Segmenting customers
3. Creating value propositions
4. Developing a sales process

Answer

Option 1: This is a correct option. Not all of the steps of analyzing the competition were carried out completely by the sales team.

Option 2: This is an incorrect option. The step of segmenting customers was not performed at all – it was overlooked completely by the team.

Option 3: This is a correct option. The value proposition created by the team does not fulfill all the criteria. While it identifies the patients' needs and problems, and specifies what the unique solution is, it isn't geared to the actual customers – doctors and hospitals.

Option 4: This is an incorrect option. All seven steps of developing a sales process were carried out well.

Case Study: Question 3 of 3

How could the competition have been better analyzed?

Options:

1. The team should have listed indirect competition as well as potential competition

2. The team should have identified all possible competitors' strengths and weaknesses

3. The team should have gathered extensive information on all possible competitors

4. The team should have segmented customers to identify potential competitors

Answer

Option 1: This is an incorrect option. The team did in fact list all the businesses that address the same customer needs, which includes primary, secondary, and potential competitors.

Sales Foundation

Option 2: This is a correct option. The team should have determined the strengths and weaknesses of all the company's competitors, not just the primary one.

Option 3: This is a correct option. The team should have investigated all of the competition, finding out everything possible about every company, not just the closest rival.

Option 4: This is an incorrect option. The team did in fact overlook customer segmentation, but performing segmentation would not help in analyzing the competition.

The sales team at the pharmaceutical company has some room to improve when developing a sales strategy. The team identified all the company's competitors, but only gathered information on and determined strengths and weaknesses of the primary competition, not all the competitors. Team members overlooked the step of segmenting customers. That didn't help when they created the value proposition, which was not geared to the right target market. However, the team did a good job of crafting a seven-step sales process.

CHAPTER 3 - Preparing for Successful Sales

Developing a Sales Presentation
Delivering a Sales Presentation
Negotiating and Handling Objections
Closing a Sale

Developing a Sales Presentation

Good presentations are customized. They include information relevant to the customer, connect the customer to the product, and include case studies and testimonials that resonate with the customer. Brochures or pamphlets – leave-behinds – are also important, as they give customers something to remember you by.

Each part of a presentation – introduction, body, and closing – has a specific function, which determines the kind of information that belongs there.

Gathering information

Sales presentations are vital tools in the selling process. Given their importance, you'd think that salespeople would have perfected the art of the presentation, wouldn't you? Unfortunately, this isn't the case.

There are a multitude of bad presentation practices. Some presenters simply read the text off their overhead slides, making for a boring delivery.

Other presenters don't take questions until the end of their presentations. This denies audience members a chance to clarify areas of confusion or dig deeper into areas of interest.

Still others rely on "canned" presentations – that is, they develop one presentation and deliver it to all their customer groups.

You don't want to deliver a bad presentation. So, what makes a good one? Preparation is key. Researching and gathering the right information go a long way toward ensuring that your presentation will engage your audience and result in a sale.

Preparation begins with gathering background information. Learn all you can about your product, your potential customers, your company's history, the market for the product, and the strengths and weaknesses of your competition.

Sales Foundation

Your product

To learn enough to explain and answer questions, you must become an expert. Assume your audience knows nothing about you, your company, or your product. Learn everything you can from the basics to the fine points.

Potential customers

Learn as much as you can about your potential customers – their organization's mission, how long they've been in business, and who their major clients are.

Your company's history

Customers will want to know about your company – how long it's been in business, what its growth record is, and its values and ethics.

The market

Learn about your potential customers' industry and their markets. Be prepared to show potential customers how your product can help them meet their goals in the marketplace.

Strengths and weaknesses of competition

Research your competition's strengths and weaknesses. You'll want to compare and contrast ways your product measures up. Be careful not to denigrate the competition, though. This can backfire.

Customizing the sales presentation

As you do your research, think about how you're going to "customize your pitch." Each group of potential customers has unique needs and wants, time frames, and budgetary constraints. To deliver a successful presentation, you must deliver only the information each group needs in ways its members can understand.

There are three basic strategies for customizing your pitch:
- • make the presentation relevant to each customer group,
- connect your product to the customer, and
- include case studies, testimonials, and examples that are relevant and meaningful for the customer.

Make presentation relevant

Don't deliver a "canned" presentation. Instead, talk to customers and find out what their needs and problems really are. Select information that outlines how your product resolves those concerns.

As a tip, an easy way to show customers that your presentation is focused on their needs is to put their company name or logo on your presentation slides.

Sales Foundation

Connect product to customer

Connect your product to your customers by stressing the benefits that apply specifically to them. Show how the product will reduce costs, for instance, or how it will make a customer's operation more efficient. Address how your product is superior to the competition's.

You may also want to bring a sample product for the customer to handle. If you can't bring the actual product, bring a model or computer prototype.

Include case studies and testimonials

Good case studies and testimonials are useful for illustrating how your product addresses specific needs. If you don't have good case studies or examples, consider canvassing your existing clients for positive experiences they have had with your product.

Another important element to consider for your presentation is the leave-behind. Don't walk away from a presentation without leaving a sales brochure or a booklet for the customer to remember you by. Your leave-behinds should be engaging and have a professional look and feel.

There are some dos and don'ts associated with leave-behinds. Do make a good impression by having your materials professionally created and bound. Have them printed on heavy, high-quality stock. Use semi-gloss, not glossy, paper, and full-color printing. Include images. Don't leave behind copies of all your slides stapled together. This shows a lack of preparation, and most customers would likely just throw these away.

Question

Which statements describe general considerations for customizing pitch and gathering presentation materials?

Options:

1. One presentation should be created, containing all of the information customers commonly want

2. Presentations must be tailored, so they're relevant to each group of customers

3. One good story that applies universally to all situations should be developed

4. The product must be connected to the customer by such strategies as putting the customer's logo or company name on presentation slides

5. After the presentation, copies of all of your presentation slides should be distributed

6. A professionally printed and bound booklet or brochure should be created as a leave-behind

Sales Foundation

Answer

Option 1: This option isn't correct. A single presentation likely won't address the specific needs of each potential customer.

Option 2: This option is correct. Customers have unique needs and concerns that can only be addressed by customizing your presentation.

Option 3: This option isn't correct. It's unlikely there's a single story that addresses all situations. Instead, collect stories and examples and use the ones that apply to particular customers.

Option 4: This option is correct. Putting the customer's logo or company name on presentation slides shows that you are focused on that particular customer's situation.

Option 5: This option isn't correct. Copies of presentation slides usually end up in a desk drawer or the trash bin. A leave-behind should be well thought out and professionally done.

Option 6: This option is correct. A leave-behind should be something the customer wants to keep. Creating a booklet or brochure and having it professionally done shows you value your product, and the customer likely will too.

Organizing the sales presentation

A great deal of research and data-gathering goes into planning a presentation. To stay organized and choose the appropriate information, it's helpful to consider how information fits within the presentation structure – the introduction, body, and closing.

The introduction should focus on the customer's needs and your product's benefits. You should also provide information about yourself and your company. This helps establish credibility.

It may be important to provide an accurate and realistic time frame for product delivery in the introduction, if this is an issue for the client.

When you present your information, don't oversell or overpromise. You want to establish a long-term relationship with customers. This is impossible if you promise what you can't deliver.

Consider Charlie, a long-time sales associate with a manufacturing firm. Charlie's company has been in business for 45 years selling ball bearings to aircraft companies. The company has an excellent reputation in the industry for safety and fast delivery. Now the company wants to diversify by selling to new markets.

Charlie is making a presentation to a skateboard

Sales Foundation

manufacturer. He's done his research, and he knows the customer could benefit from his company's new line of specially coated ball bearings. He also knows that the customer is experiencing some issues with its current supplier.

Question

Charlie opens his presentation by introducing himself and presenting his sales experience.

What other kinds of information should Charlie include?

Options:

1. Criticism of the vendor's poor quality ball bearings

2. His company's history as a reliable vendor

3. Explanation of the company's safety record and delivery policies

4. A guarantee that his ball bearings won't cause problems

Answer

Option 1: This option isn't correct. Criticizing the competition is never a good idea. It would make Charlie look bad.

Option 2: This option is correct. Customers will want to know who Charlie represents and how stable and reliable his company is.

Option 3: This option is correct. The company's

safety record is a major benefit of buying Charlie's product.

Option 4: This option isn't correct. This kind of a guarantee might be overselling, since problems could arise.

After the introduction comes the body of the presentation. The body provides detailed information about the product's features and benefits.

It's important to balance thoroughness and brevity in the body. Too much information could confuse customers and delay a buying decision. Too little could cause the customer to dismiss the product altogether.

Be as succinct as possible. Remember that people are sitting and listening while you speak; fatigue can set in quickly.

In addition to information about features, the body of the presentation must give verifiable statistics that support the benefits of your product. For instance, cost savings, increased productivity, or reduced downtime statistics collected from your customer database can indicate how your product would favorably affect the customer's bottom line.

A third critical piece of information to include in the body is your product's costs. These must be

Sales Foundation

provided accurately and in detail – they're a primary consideration in whether or not the customer will buy. For a complicated project or product, costs should be broken down to show each development or implementation stage. And remember to include "hidden costs," such as travel and administrative expenses or required maintenance.

Question

Remember Charlie at the manufacturing firm? He's planning the body of his presentation.

What kinds of information should Charlie include in the body of his presentation?

Options:

1. Costs of the specially coated ball bearings in the size the customer would use

2. Statistics on failure rates of his company's ball bearings

3. Costs of all the ball bearing lines the company makes

4. Specifications and tolerances for the recommended ball bearings

5. Savings resulting from a reduction in skateboard replacements due to bearing failure 6. Information about how the global ball bearing industry is growing

Answer

Sorin Dumitrascu

Option 1: This option is correct. Charlie needs to provide detailed costs, including any hidden costs associated with the ball bearings.

Option 2: This option is correct. These statistics are important, especially when they're favorable to Charlie's company.

Option 3: This option is incorrect. This is too much information. Charlie knows the size of bearings the customer needs, so only those costs are necessary.

Option 4: This option is correct. Detailed information about the product should be included in the body of the presentation, although detail should be balanced with brevity.

Option 5: This option is correct. Information about savings shows how Charlie's product will favorably affect the customer's bottom line.

Option 6: This option is incorrect. A discussion about the growth of the ball bearing industry could be interesting, but it will not necessarily help Charlie make the sale.

The final component of the presentation structure is the closing. The closing is your last chance to sell the product. For this reason, you must refocus attention to the product's benefits and summarize how the product meets the customer's

Sales Foundation

needs.

Part of the closing is the "call to action" – a statement or question that motivates the customer to take the next step toward closing. In a sense, the call to action is the most important part of the presentation – it's where you begin to get some pay-off for your efforts.

Question

Match types of information with the parts of the presentation to which they belong. Each part may have more than one match.

Options:

A. Detailed discussion of product benefits
B. Call to action
C. Discussion of customer's needs
D. History of salesperson's company
E. Product or project's costs
F. How product affects customer's bottom line

Targets:

1. Introduction
2. Body
3. Closing

Answer

The introduction should focus on how the product meets the customer's needs. It may also feature a brief history of the salesperson's company.

Sorin Dumitrascu

The body is a detailed discussion of product benefits, an outline of costs, and statistics that show how the product affects the customer's bottom line.

The closing summarizes the benefits of the product for this customer, and contains a call to action to encourage the customer to take the next step in the sales process.

Delivering a Sales Presentation

To deliver a presentation successfully, you must rehearse. Be sure to use a coach. Don't forget to rehearse using your slides and reference aids, and practice operating the equipment you'll use during the presentation.

When delivering a presentation, ask questions and take notes. Get to the point and focus on the customer. Practice active listening. Be honest and consistent. Be animated and dramatic. Use a flipchart, whiteboard, or pad of paper. And show belief in your product.

Rehearsing the presentation

Imagine that you've spent weeks preparing a sales presentation. You've researched the prospect extensively, you know what the prospect's needs and problems are, and you've developed an excellent presentation. But when you begin to deliver the presentation, your nerves get the better of you. Information doesn't flow, your case studies aren't engaging, you fumble with your slides, and you end up being less effective than you'd hoped.

Speaking in front of strangers can be daunting. But there is something you can do that will make the task easier – rehearse. Ask someone you trust to rehearse with you. This should be a disinterested third party who won't be attending the presentation. This coach observes you, often taking notes, and provides feedback on your pacing, the volume and tone of your voice, the clarity of your word choices, and how engaging your presentation is.

If possible, it's a good idea to rehearse in the room where you'll give the actual presentation. This enables you to practice how you'll move. For instance, if you'll be moving from a chair to a podium, practice doing it. You want to look smooth and confident on presentation day.

Practice using your notes. Losing your place and

Sales Foundation

fumbling with note cards looks unprofessional. Get familiar with the equipment you'll be using for the presentation. Call the customer to find out what kind of equipment will be provided. Then, learn to use it seamlessly. The more you practice, the more confident you'll be. On the other hand, too much rehearsal can rob your delivery of spontaneity. Try not to memorize your presentation, or else it might sound stale.

Question

Rehearsing offers numerous benefits. What do you suppose some of the benefits are?

Options:

1. You'll be able to change words or phrases that sound awkward when spoken aloud
2. You'll be able to adjust your pacing
3. You'll improve your confidence
4. You'll be able to memorize the presentation more easily
5. Your presentation will engage the audience and result in a sale

Answer

Option 1: This option is correct. What reads well doesn't always sound good aloud. Rehearsing enables you to smooth out your wording for maximum clarity.

Option 2: This option is correct. Some content requires more time to be spent on it than other content. Rehearsing helps you identify where you need to concentrate your time, and where you can speed up.

Option 3: This option is correct. The more you rehearse, the more confident you'll be that the actual presentation will be a success.

Option 4: This option is not correct. If you memorize your presentation, it may sound uninspired. Know your information, and try to sound spontaneous each time you present.

Option 5: This option is not correct. Rehearsal increases the likelihood that the presentation will be more engaging, but that doesn't guarantee a sale.

Delivering the presentation

In addition to rehearsing, there are some guidelines that can help you deliver your presentation effectively:

- stay focused on the customer and get to the point,
- ask questions and take notes,
- believe in your product,
- be honest and consistent,
- be animated and engaging, and
- use a flipchart, whiteboard, or notepad.

Stay focused on customer; get to the point

Don't waste the customer's time. Keep the presentation focused on the customer's needs. Know what your key points are and make them quickly.

Ask questions and take notes

Ask questions to find out what customers actually want or need, and take notes as they speak. If you know what the customer needs, you're more likely to provide the right solution.

Believe in your product

Your words, facial expressions, and body language should reflect enthusiasm for your product.

Be honest and consistent

Nothing means more than your word. Be honest, even if it costs you the sale. Be consistent from one part of your presentation to another. If you mention a specific time frame or price, don't change it in another part of the presentation, for instance.

Be animated and engaging

Keep your customers interested by modulating your tone of voice and being animated. Use dramatic pauses for effect. Be sure your body language is open and friendly.

Use a flipchart, whiteboard, or notepad

Use a flipchart or whiteboard to note major points, draw diagrams, and write down facts and figures to emphasize them. Take notes on a notepad so you remember key points.

Another important guideline is to practice active listening. This assures your customers that you're paying attention and empathizing with what they're saying. For example, say "I understand" periodically.

Repeat back what customers say, and verify with "Yes, that's right." Rephrase customers' statements as questions. And phrase questions to achieve a tentative commitment in the customer's answer.

Say "I understand"

Using phrases like "I understand," "I see," or "uh huh" reassures the person that you're listening, and encourages the person to keep speaking.

Repeat back what customers say

For example, in response to a customer who is arguing for including additional features in a new IT project, you might say, "I hear you saying that the scope of the project isn't large enough." The customer could then verify your statement.

Rephrase statement as question

For example, a customer might say, "We need a company that can handle the job from start to finish." In response, you could say, "So what you're saying is you want a company that can move you from idea to prototype to product?"

Phrase questions to achieve customer commitment

This is a useful technique for getting an aggressive customer on your side. It can help move a potential sale toward closing.

For example, a customer might say, "We require training for 100 staff members by no later than the end of next month." You might say, "So, if I can train 100 of your staff members by the end of next month, we have a deal?"

To observe these guidelines in action, consider

an example. Meet Travis, an agent for a leading insurance company. Travis has been working on several new personal lines accounts, and now he's delivering his sales presentation to Raheem and Sarah.

Travis begins his presentation by introducing himself and his company. Follow along as Travis continues his presentation.

Travis: The reason I'm here today isn't to sell you anything. I'm here to give you information and listen to your questions and concerns. Once we've talked, you can decide whether you want to buy what I'm selling. How does that sound to you?

Sarah: Sounds good, Travis. We appreciate your concern for our time.

Travis: Let's begin by talking about your specific needs. And I'm going to take notes on what you tell me. So why do you think you need to buy insurance?

Raheem: Well, we've just bought a new house. I've been lying awake at night worrying about all the crazy things that can happen – fire, flood, hurricane damage, tornados. I want to know that if something happens, we'll be taken care of.

Travis: I hear you saying that you want peace of mind. Is that right?

Sales Foundation

Sarah: Right. Another thing we want is protection against loss. Everything we have is tied up in this house. I want to know that if something happens, we'd be able to recover financially and move on.

Travis: So, Sarah, you're looking for financial security?

Sarah: Yes.

Travis: Well, suppose I were to tell you that I can provide both peace of mind and security immediately, for no money. What would you think?

Raheem: Let's keep talking.

Question

So far in this presentation, Travis has let his potential customers do most of the talking.

Which guidelines has Travis observed correctly?

Options:

1. Ask questions and take notes
2. Focus on the customer
3. Practice active listening
4. Be honest and consistent
5. Urge the customer to buy
6. Provide detailed prices

Answer

Option 1: This option is correct. Travis finds out what Raheem and Sarah are interested in by asking them questions. He notes their answers on a pad of paper.

Option 2: This option is correct. Travis doesn't waste any time; he focuses directly on Raheem's and Sarah's needs.

Option 3: This option is correct. Travis repeats back what each person says to him and asks for verification. This shows Raheem and Sarah that Travis truly hears what they're saying.

Option 4: This option is correct. Travis is honest about his product when he says that no one really wants to buy insurance. This technique relaxes his customers and helps them trust Travis.

Option 5: This option is not correct. Travis doesn't use any pressure tactics. He asks questions and listens. In fact, Travis's customers do most of the talking.

Option 6: This option is not correct. Travis doesn't go into any detail in this part of the presentation. He focuses on the customers and their needs.

Next, Travis goes on to explain details of his company's homeowner's insurance policy, including coverage and costs. Follow along as he discusses the details with Raheem and Sarah.

Sales Foundation

Travis: Let's talk coverage first. Since yours is a new house, I recommend covering it for its replacement cost. This means that if a disaster occurs, and you lose the house, you'll be able to rebuild this same house, with the same finishes.

Raheem: But, Travis, the housing market is volatile and changes frequently. How do you keep track of what the house is worth?

Travis: Replacement cost is based on costs of materials and labor, not on market value. Say it cost $100,000 to build this house. You could sell it for $200,000, but we're not buying your house. If the house burned down tomorrow, we'd send you a check for $100,000 so you could rebuild this very house.

Sarah: Does it cover anything else? Lots of things can happen to a house that don't involve replacing the entire structure.

Travis: Well, a client called me up last month. Her pipes had frozen and burst, and her finished basement was flooded. This woman had expensive carpeting and silk-upholstered furniture that was completely ruined. Her daughter was getting married in two weeks, and she was planning to hold the reception in this room. She was completely hysterical.

Travis: We sent an agent to assess the damage,

and he cut a check on the same day. The client was able to repaint and replace everything in time to go ahead with her plans for the reception.

Raheem: Where do I sign up?

Travis: Well, let's talk prices and deductibles. I want to get you the right coverage at the lowest possible cost. Then we'll send an appraiser out to evaluate your house. How does that sound?

Sarah: Fantastic. I'm so glad we kept our appointment with you! I thought you'd be a really high-pressure salesman, but you've been so helpful.

Travis: As I said at the start, I'm here to provide information. The rest is up to you. Here's a packet of information. I'll make notes for you as we talk.

Question

Which guidelines has Travis followed in this part of his presentation?

Options:

1. He's animated and dramatic
2. He shows he believes in his product
3. He de-emphasizes prices and costs
4. He promises what he knows he can't deliver
5. He uses a whiteboard, flipchart, or pad of paper

Answer

Option 1: This option is correct. Travis

Sales Foundation

modulates his voice effectively and acts dramatically in telling his story about the woman with the flood-damaged basement.

Option 2: This option is correct. Travis shows his belief in his company in talking about its excellent service.

Option 3: This option isn't correct. Travis makes a point of talking about costs.

Option 4: This option isn't correct. Travis is selling a valuable product that he believes in.

Option 5: This option is correct. Travis uses a pad of paper to emphasize key points.

Case Study: Question 1 of 1
Scenario
Answer the question.
Question
Which guidelines did Beth use correctly in delivering her presentation?
Options:
1. She was honest and consistent
2. She showed belief in her product
3. She practiced active listening
4. She focused on the customer and got to the point
5. She used a whiteboard, flipchart, or pad of paper

6. She asked questions and took notes

7. She was animated and dramatic

Answer

Option 1: This option is not correct. Beth wasn't honest. When asked whether she could deliver the product by July, she guaranteed delivery without knowing whether the team could meet the deadline or not.

Option 2: This option is correct. Beth was enthusiastic and clearly believes in the product she's selling.

Option 3: This option isn't correct. Beth didn't practice any of the active listening techniques. In fact, she deflected her audience's questions.

Option 4: This option isn't correct. Beth didn't get to the point. Instead, she indulged herself by explaining one of the games in detail.

Option 5: This option is correct. Beth used visual aids, as well as the flipchart for her cost presentation.

Option 6: This option isn't correct. Rather than ask the administrators what they needed or wanted, Beth launched into an explanation of her product.

Option 7: This option is correct. Beth used images and roleplayed one of the activities.

Negotiating and Handling Objections

Handling objections and negotiations are two important elements of the sales process.

Objections are hurdles that stand between you and closing the sale. There are four main types of objections: price, competition, "will it work?" and "not now." Knowing how to overcome objections will help you achieve your negotiating goals.

There are two sets of guidelines for negotiating a sale. One set concerns how you should act: be patient, listen to the customer, use effective body language, and use appropriate humor. The other set of guidelines concerns actions or statements related to the point being negotiated. These guidelines include: don't offer the bottom line too early; let customers make the first offer; get something in return for added value; and know when to walk away.

Preparing to negotiate

How many times have you heard, "You'll have to do better than that," or "We're not in the market right now," or "We already buy from your competition?" These kinds of statements are called objections – they're hurdles that stand in the way of making sales. Looked at another way, though, objections are invitations to negotiate.

Selling and negotiating are closely linked. During the sales process, you'll constantly probe for information to use later, when negotiating price, terms, quality, and delivery of your product.

The actual negotiations occur during the discovery phase of the developing step of the sales process. It's during this step that you begin to discover the problems and objections that customers have to your solution.

Negotiation involves considerable give-and-take. You may not get everything you want, but you may be able to get more than you think. There are some guidelines that can help you prepare for a successful negotiation:

- • Ask for more than you want.
- Do your homework – anticipate the demands of the other side.
- Determine what you want from the

negotiation. Prioritize your wants, so you'll make the right trade-offs.
- Find out about relationships among your customers; identify the decision makers. These are the people who have the power to say "yes" or "no."
- Be prepared to compromise and work toward a solution that's satisfactory to everyone.

Negotiation is tricky and often tiring. It's important to project confidence in yourself and your solution. You must know your bottom line, and recognize when the deal on the table is the best one you can achieve. Patience and persistence pay off, but don't be afraid to walk away. It's often better to lose a sale than to give up too much.

Question

Which statements are guidelines that can help when you're preparing to negotiate a sale?

Options:

1. Ask for more than you want at the start
2. Work toward a mutually agreeable solution
3. Overpromise, so the customer will agree to your solution
4. Find out who has the power to say "yes" or "no"
5. Distinguish your "must haves" from your

"nice to haves"

6. Give customers what they ask for

7. Anticipate the needs and wants of the other side

Answer

Option 1: This option is correct. It's difficult to get more during a negotiation if you start off by asking for less than what you really want. So aim high – it will give you room to bargain.

Option 2: This option is correct. You must be prepared to compromise and work toward defining a solution both you and the customer can be happy with.

Option 3: This option isn't correct. If you overpromise, you may get caught having to explain why you cannot deliver.

Option 4: This option is correct. It may be that only one or two of your customers are empowered to make a deal with you. Find out who they are, so you don't spend time negotiating with people who aren't authorized to close the sale.

Option 5: This option is correct. Separating "must haves" from "nice to haves" gives you room to bargain. You'll know what you must fight for, and what you can let go.

Option 6: This option isn't correct. Like you, customers will aim high and ask for everything. You must bargain with them, identify what they really need, and work toward a mutually satisfactory agreement.

Option 7: This option is correct. Identifying what the other side wants enables you to anticipate their arguments. Then you'll be better able to craft your own arguments and responses.

Countering objections

During the sales process, your customers will be working to achieve the best prices and terms possible. They'll be raising objections that prevent you from closing the sale. You need to be able to recognize objections and counter them successfully.

Customers express objections in many different ways, but they all boil down to variations on four basic themes: price, competition, "will it work?" and "not now."

The price objection is the one you'll likely need to counter most often. Customers rarely if ever accept the first price offered in a negotiation.

There are two methods to counter the price objection. One is to emphasize the value of your product; the other is to explain how your product offers the lowest total cost of ownership. For example, suppose you're selling kitchen appliances to a buyer for a new hotel. Your customer says, "I like everything you're telling me except for the price." What do you do?

Emphasize value

High-priced products often have features and benefits that low-cost products don't have. For example, in response to the price objection for your appliances, you could say, "Our prices include the best warranty in the industry. We also provide 24-7 service capability."

Offer lowest total cost of ownership

Two pieces of equipment may look and function relatively the same ways, but one may last longer and cost less to operate in the long run. It has the lower total cost of ownership. So, in response to the price objection, you could say, "Our appliances last twice as long as the competition's, with fewer repairs over the life of the appliance."

A second type of objection you'll encounter is the competition objection. Suppose you're trying to sell auto parts to Mariana. She says, "Sorry. We buy all our auto parts from Phil." This means Mariana already has a supplier that she's happy with.

What can you say? You don't want to get into a point-by-point comparison between your product and the competition's product. The customer likely knows the benefits and drawbacks of the chosen vendor. Nor do you want to criticize or bad-mouth the competition. This would just annoy the customer and make you look bad.

Instead, try to find out about the competition's product. You may be able to counter the objection with one of two approaches: offer the customer a complementary product or service, or supplement the competition's product or service in some way.

Offer a complementary product or service

Say you sell floor cleaning and sanitizing services, but your potential customer already has a floor-cleaning service. You could find out whether the competition's service includes sanitizing. If it doesn't, you may be able to sell your service as a complement to the competition's service.

Supplement the competition's product or service

You may be able to offer a supplemental service to the competition's floor-cleaning service. For example, you could offer spot cleaning for high-traffic areas if the competition doesn't provide it. In this case, you'd come in after the competition has cleaned the floors to perform your supplemental service.

Another objection is "will it work?" This objection often springs from a customer's prior bad experience with your product, a similar product, or your company.

If a customer has been dissatisfied with your company in the past, it may be impossible for you to make a sale during this initial meeting. However,

Sales Foundation

you may still be able to pave the way for a future sale.

Consider Mark, a salesman for a technology company. He's visiting Denise, the director of a health care agency. Mark wants Denise to buy his company's new telephone system, but Denise has had a bad prior experience with Mark's company. Follow along as Mark counters her objection.

Denise: I almost canceled our meeting, Mark. The last time we dealt with your company, we had nothing but problems. The phone system was down more than it was operational. We lost a lot of money and client goodwill.

Mark: I understand. We fired the team that developed that system, and we've replaced all of that technology with the latest technology, equipment, and expertise.

Denise: Too late for us.

Mark: I'll give you the names and numbers of several customers who experienced the same problems you did, and who now have our new systems installed. One of the customers is a health care agency like yours. These customers have saved thousands of dollars.

Denise: Well, I won't promise anything, but if we can save money, I'll make the phone calls.

Sorin Dumitrascu

Denise pauses before she speaks.

Mark deals with Denise's "will it work?" objection in three ways. He sympathizes with her. He tells her about improvements in his company and his product. Then he provides names and numbers of people who have benefited from his product. While Mark probably can't persuade Denise to buy his product, the people whose phone numbers he provides may convince her to purchase.

The final objection type is "not now." This objection indicates that customers don't need your product. You may hear, "Thanks for calling, but we're not in the market at the moment."

There really is no way to counter this objection. However, the customer could be in the market for your product at a later date. You should leave some sales literature behind and ask for permission to call again. If the customer agrees, ask when you should call back.

Negotiating a sale

Countering objections can be part of negotiating with the customer to obtain the best price and terms. Some people are born negotiators, but most people have to learn how.

Two sets of guidelines can help you become more effective at negotiating. The first set concerns how you should act during a negotiation. The second set concerns statements and actions that relate to the point being negotiated.

The way you act can have a profound effect on your results. There are some important behavior guidelines to observe:

- use effective body language,
- listen when the customer speaks,
- be patient, and
- use humor, when it's appropriate.

Your customers will be observing you carefully during negotiations. They'll watch for opportunities to press an advantage; they'll observe you for signs of fatigue or distraction. You need to control your body language to ensure you're sending the appropriate messages.

Body language can also be used strategically. For instance, imagine you've been negotiating price with a client for several hours. The customer throws out a price that isn't a serious offer. Rather than address the offer verbally, you look off into the distance, frown, and shrug. Noticing your reaction, the customer quickly offers an explanation and a new price.

Another important behavior is to listen carefully when the customer speaks. Listening encompasses both what the customer says and how the person acts. For instance, is the prospect hesitant? Are there signs of irritation or impatience? What is the person's body language telling you?

Listening is important

As you may have noted, when customers speak, they may reveal information that will give you an advantage, a weakness you can exploit, or an area of similarity that you can use to create rapport. Listening enables you to continually adjust your negotiating tactics to suit the people with whom you're dealing.

Another important behavior is to be patient. You need time to process information, and the customer does too. If you show a customer you're anxious to make a deal, the customer may decide to hold out and wait for you to offer concessions.

The important concessions tend to happen

during the last minutes of a negotiation anyway, so be patient as negotiations evolve.

The last behavior guideline is to use humor, if it seems appropriate. Humor is tricky – it can offend people. However, humor can also defuse tension, surprise people and get them to take a different approach, and ease the way forward. Humor nearly always lightens the mood of a negotiation.

Question

Elliott is a regional account executive with a national direct mail service provider. He's meeting with Jim from an electronics supply company to negotiate the terms of a deal.

Which behavior-related guidelines does Elliott use in his negotiation?

Options:

1. Be patient
2. Use body language
3. Use humor

Answer

Option 1: This option isn't correct. Elliott is impatient to make the deal. He launches into a discussion of terms before giving his customer time to ask questions.

Option 2: This is the correct option. Elliott's body language echoes his vocal enthusiasm.

Furthermore, his strategic flinch, when Jim offers a low price, conveys meaning better than words could.

Option 3: This option is incorrect. Elliott doesn't use humor in this negotiation.

A second set of guidelines that are important in learning to negotiate are associated with statements or actions related to the point under negotiation:
don't offer your bottom line too early
let customers make the first offer
get something in return for added value, and
know when to walk away

Sometimes, out of fear of losing a deal or as a result of inexperience, a negotiator offers the bottom line too early in the proceedings. If this happens, the negotiator has no room to bargain. Recognizing the mistake, customers will likely press for more concessions.

It's important not to offer your best deal too quickly. Be patient and don't panic. If the customer demands your best price, name a higher price than what you expect to get. Aiming high gives you room to maneuver. You may end up with more than you'd hoped to get.

A related guideline is to let your customers make the first offer. You may be tempted to jump in, but you're better off waiting. The customer's offer could be higher than you were expecting.

As a bargaining ploy, negotiators sometimes "sweeten the pot" by offering extra support or services that add value to their main product or service. If you do this, remember to get something in return. Don't give away valuable services.

For example, the customer may say, "I agree that those special services you keep bringing up would be nice, but we simply don't have the funds for them. Could you include them at no additional cost?"

If you decide to waive the cost of the extra services, at least use the free services as leverage when negotiating the price. Giving in on the extras can help you stand firm against customer demands for price concessions.

Despite your best efforts and negotiating skills, you may come to a point when you've offered your bottom line deal, and the customer continues asking for concessions. What do you do? The answer is walk away.

When you have nothing more to offer, it's time to conclude the negotiations. Not always, but sometimes, when customers see that you're prepared to walk away from the table, they'll give in.

Sorin Dumitrascu

Question

Remember Elliott and Jim? Analyze how well Elliott applies the guidelines for statements or actions related to the point under negotiation.

Which guidelines does Elliott follow in his negotiation with Jim?

Options:

1. Know when to walk away
2. Get something back for added value
3. Let customers make the first offer
4. Don't offer your bottom line too soon

Answer

Option 1: This option is not correct. The scenario indicates that the negotiations ended satisfactorily.

Option 2: This option is correct. Elliott offers Jim the new 3-D process to use for free for a period of six months. Elliott uses this offer as an incentive for Jim to agree to contract with his company. After six months, Jim will pay for the service.

Option 3: This option is correct. Elliott got Jim to make the first offer, which Elliott then rejected.

Option 4: This option is correct. Elliott aimed high with his offer. He left himself room to bring the price down during his bargaining.

Closing a Sale

The last part of the sales process is closing the sale.

There are signs that can help you decide on the right time for closing. The pace may slow as customers think through the benefits of your product, or it may quicken as customers get excited about their intended purchase. Customers may also ask specific questions to justify spending money on your product.

There are some actions you can take to help customers make their buying decision. You can give customers a reason to buy now rather than later, help them reach the decision to buy, show customers how the product can solve their problems, and narrow the choices.

There are different types of closing. One is the invitational close, in which you invite the customer to buy. Another type of close is the directive close – you simply assume the customer is buying and present the terms of the sale.

Watching for signs and building momentum

After you've been through the negotiation stage and dealt with objections in the discovery step in the sales process, you're ready to move on to closing the sale. This is what you've been working up to all along – it's the payoff for all of the hard work that you've done. It can also be a stressful time. What if the customer says "no?" But, the more you know, the easier it will be to have a successful closing.

An important aspect of closing is to recognize when to close the sale. If you try to close too soon, customers may have no choice but to turn you down. They may not have enough information about the product, or they may not have had enough time to process everything you've told them.

On the other hand, if you wait too long to close, you give customers too much time to think about alternatives. Customers may back away from committing to the sale, or the competition might steal the customers away from you.

The point is close at the right time – when both you and your customers have all the information you and they need to make the deal.

How will you know when to close? There are signs to watch for. During the sales process, you and your customers have been getting to know each

Sales Foundation

other. You've gotten into a rhythm of giving and receiving information. A momentum has been building. As customers achieve a "critical mass" of knowledge, you may feel the pace of negotiations begin to change.

For example, the pace may slow as customers rationalize the purchase and convince themselves they're doing the right thing. Or the pace may quicken when customers have made the decision internally to purchase and the stress subsides. They may become excited or anxious. This change of pace signals that customers may be ready to make a commitment.

Another sign is that customers may begin to ask specific questions, such as, "How long would delivery take?" or "What does this button do?" These kinds of questions signify that the purchase has become real to them, and imminent.

The actions you can take to build momentum toward closing a sale are to give customers reasons to buy now rather than later, help customers reach the decision to buy, show customers how the product solves their problems, and narrow the choices.

One action you can take to build momentum is to give customers reasons why they should buy now rather than later. This gives customers an incentive to move forward. For example, you could say that the price is going up after today, or the product might not be available in sufficient quantity later on.

When you do this, however, you must be honest. Don't tell customers what isn't true. And don't push. Most customers react negatively to sales pressure.

For example, suppose you sell health club memberships. Your potential customer is unsure about joining; she isn't sure she can commit the time necessary to achieve fitness. To give this customer a reason to buy now, you could say, "If you can't commit, you may never achieve your goals. But if you commit now, I'll make sure you get a trainer who'll put you on the road to total fitness."

Another way to build momentum is to help your customers reach the decision to buy. When you sense that customers are nearing the decision point, refocus their attention on the benefits you're providing. Show them how all or most of their needs will be met.

Another way to increase momentum is to show customers how your product solves their problems. To do this, personalize the product and demonstrate how it fits into their lives, their offices, or their work flows.

Sales Foundation

How your printer solves the customer's problem

As you may have noted, one thing you could do is to show photographs of different environments in which your printers are being used. Point out how your printers fit easily into employee workstations.

Another thing you could do is help the customer visualize the size of your printers by providing the dimensions, or pointing out something in his office that is a similar size.

One problem you can help customers solve is that of affording your product. It's important to offer a variety of payment plans. For example, one plan may involve putting down a deposit and paying the balance on delivery. Another plan may provide for scheduled monthly payments. Still a third plan might require payment up front in return for a discount. You want to make it as easy as possible for your customer to say "yes" to buying your product.

The last action you can take to increase momentum is to narrow the choices that customers have. Some customers become confused when faced with too many options. If this occurs, begin eliminating options.

Start with the options that are too expensive.

Then continue with options that don't appear to be a high priority for the customer. If the customer says, "Wait, I need that," ask, "What do you like about it?" Continue trimming until you have an offering the customer understands and can agree to buy.

Question

Cary is selling a line of organic foods to Sue, a grocery store manager.

Which techniques can Cary use to increase the momentum of the sale and move it to closing?

Options:

1. Eliminate options that Sue doesn't need, so there are a manageable number to choose from
2. Refocus on the benefits of the product to help Sue make her decision
3. Tell Sue that if she buys today, she'll be eligible for a discount
4. Outline different payment plans to help Sue afford the product
5. Outline your preferred payment option and ask for payment up front
6. Gauge what Sue would be willing to pay and lower his prices

Answer

Option 1: This is a correct option. Having too many options can confuse customers. Cary needs to

Sales Foundation

narrow down the choices by eliminating options Sue doesn't need.

Option 2: This is a correct option. When Cary begins to close the sale, he must refocus on the benefits of the product so benefits are clear in Sue's mind.

Option 3: This is a correct option. Offering incentives to buy is an important technique to use in closing a sale.

Option 4: This is a correct option. Flexibility in payment options is important. It means that customers who have varying budgets can afford the product.

Option 5: This option isn't correct. Cary should provide Sue with payment options and help her choose the one that meets her budget.

Option 6: This option isn't correct. Instead of lowering the price, Cary should offer incentives, such as a discount or a value-added feature.

Choosing a closing method

Once you've established that customers are ready to make the purchasing decision, your next step is to ask for the sale. If you don't do this, you likely won't get the sale. After listening to your presentation, the customer may say, "This all sounds great, but I need to think about it. Let me get back to you."

What are the odds that the customer will call you back? Slim to none. Before you leave the negotiating table for the last time, you must be direct and ask the customer to buy your product.

When you sense that the time is right to close, you present what's called a trial close. A good trial close might be, "Do you have any more questions or concerns about what I've told you?" If the customer says "no," you proceed with your closing.

There are many different types of closing. The ones you adopt as your own depend upon your personality, the nature of the rapport that you establish with customers, and perhaps the tone of the negotiation itself. For example, you may choose to use a simple, natural technique, such as the invitational close, or a more forceful method, such as the directive close.

The invitational close provides a gentle nudge toward taking action. For example, you may say, "If you like what I've shown you, why don't you give it a try?" or, "How about it? Are you ready to sign on the dotted line?"

The invitational close is successful because customers may not be able to think of any reason for not buying; they'll often commit to the sale.

Another type of close is the directive close. This close is more forceful than the invitational close. It diverts the customer's thinking away from the purchasing decision, to the ownership and enjoyment of the product.

With a directive close, you simply assume the customer is buying your product. When the customer answers "no" to "Do you have any more questions?", you simply proceed to the next step in the sales process. For instance, you may say, "Great. I'll need your signature on these two forms and a check for $3,000."

The advantage of the directive close is that you keep control of the conversation. Customers don't have the opportunity to back away, equivocate, or start thinking about your competition's offer.

Question

Match types of closing methods with their characteristics. Each method matches to more than one characteristic.

Options:

A. Directive
B. Invitational

Targets:

1. You assume the customer is buying the product
2. You provide a gentle nudge to buy the product
3. You keep the initiative and control of the conversation
4. You ask the customer to buy
5. You tell the customer what the next steps in the buying process are

Answer

With the directive close, you don't ask for the sale; you simply assume the customer is going to buy the product.

The invitational close enables you to nudge the customer to buy the product. It is less forceful than the directive close but just as effective.

The directive close enables you to keep control of the conversation and guide it toward the next steps.

The invitational close involves a question asking the customer to purchase the product.

The directive close enables you to guide the purchasing process and tell the customer what steps come next.

CHAPTER 4 - Developing Strong Customer Relationships

Getting to Know Your Customer
Establishing Effective Communication
Building Credibility with Customers
Practice: Establishing Credibility

Getting to Know Your Customer

By establishing a strong customer relationship, a salesperson can become a more effective seller. Recognizing the needs of the customer is a core aim for any selling organization. Salespeople should know the following about their customers: who they are, what they buy, why they buy, how they use the product or service, and what they really think of the seller.

Competent sellers strive to understand what category their current customers are in. This allows them to provide specific customer care, depending on what type of customer is being dealt with. There are six different types of customers: external, internal, high value, repeat, former, and vanishing.

Customer value can be defined as the level of benefit the customer gets from a product compared to the price of the product. Customers recognize three main sources of value: the product and services solutions, the company, and the people.

What you need to know about customers

The relationship between a salesperson and a customer is a business relationship from which both parties seek to benefit. The salesperson wants to make a sale, while the customer wants a product or service. But for this relationship to be mutually beneficial, the salesperson must make an effort to learn about the customer. Although the relationship is essentially commercial in nature, its foundation is built on social interaction.

Forging relationships with customers allows salespeople to demonstrate that they are willing to discover a customer's problems and work toward providing solutions.

By showing a genuine interest in getting to know the customer, a salesperson conveys the organization's appreciation of both current and prospective customers.

Recognizing the needs of the customer is a core aim for any selling organization. It helps create an atmosphere where the customer is valued and may greatly increase the seller's chances of making a successful sale. There are some key details that salespeople should know about their customers: who they are, what they buy, why they buy it, how they use the product or service, and what they really think of the seller.

Who they are

It's important for a selling organization to build an accurate profile of its customers. If the organization sells directly to individuals, the gender, age, and occupation of the customers should be identified. If the organization is selling to another business, the type of industry and company size should be determined.

What they buy

Sellers can use information about customers' purchases to offer other services that support the initial purchase. Salespeople can also use customers' buying history to sell new products and services to them.

Why they buy

Understanding why a customer buys a product helps a seller to identify the needs of the customer. The seller can then begin selecting products from its inventory to provide solutions for the customer.

How they use the product or service

By determining how a customer uses a product or service, a company can begin to anticipate what the customer might need in the future. The seller might also be able to identify ways for the customer to further maximize the potential of the product or service.

What they really think of the seller

Feedback is important for all industries. It's particularly important for salespeople, as reputation is a crucial selling tool. Sellers need to know if customers enjoy dealing with them, and feel that they receive value for money. A selling organization can only address problems if it can identify them. This is the main reason why it's vital to understand what a customer's perception of the seller is.

The different types of customers

Salespeople define a customer as a person or organization that they believe can benefit from the product or service they are selling. Salespeople are constantly looking for prospective customers – it's an essential part of their role. However, in terms of generating sales revenue, it's dangerous to neglect existing customers while pursuing new ones.

It's not unusual to find 20% of a company's customers providing 50% of the company's revenue through repeat purchases. This is why the conscientious seller should categorize current customers. Then, the seller can provide specific customer care based upon the characteristics of the customer's category.

There are six general categories into which customers may fall:
- • external customers purchase a product or service from the seller and are not affiliated with the organization,
- internal customers include anyone within an organization, such as individuals or colleagues in different departments and branches,
- high-value customers are very important for selling companies, and are usually less

sensitive to price issues,
- repeat customers are satisfied with what the selling organization has to offer in terms of product and customer service,
- former customers who no longer wish to do business with the seller for any number of reasons, and
- vanishing customers often express interest in making significant purchases and consume valuable selling hours, only to abruptly pull out of the sale.

External customers

Since external customers are outside the company, they have financial autonomy. If they're not satisfied with a product, they'll purchase from a different seller. To retain external customers, sellers need to provide an excellent product and back it up with high-quality customer service.

For example, a purchasing officer for a government department signs a contract to purchase printer cartridges from a stationery supply company. Because the official has no connection with the company, he's considered to be an external customer.

Internal customers

If salespeople want to successfully sell to an

external customer, their relationships with internal customers must be strong. It's the efforts of internal customers that ultimately result in the product the salesperson will sell.

For example, Sarah is a salesperson working for a furniture manufacturer. She signs a contract for a large number of dining room chairs. To successfully carry out the order, she needs to have a good relationship with the Manufacturing and Dispatch departments, her internal customers. If either department fails to carry out its role, Sarah will have to make excuses to the customer for the delay. To avoid this, she conveys the importance of the order and communicates frequently with each department.

High-value customers

High-value customers are likely to make large-volume purchases, and often give referrals and provide sales leads. They also communicate well with sellers and often point out potential problems with a product.

For instance, a waste treatment plant purchases a large volume of valves from a manufacturer. A recent shipment of valves seemed to exhibit weaknesses, which led to long process delays. The treatment plant immediately notifies the company it purchased the valves from so that the manufacturer could be informed of the lapse in quality.

Sales Foundation

Repeat customers

There's a sales maxim that says it costs up to five times as much to replace a customer as it does to actually keep one. So, repeat customers are a source of solid revenue. The key to retaining this kind of customer is to underpromise and overdeliver.

John is an example of a repeat customer. He consistently returns to the same insurance broker for all his insurance needs, including car, house, and health insurance. He does so because he appreciates the level of customer service and likes the no-pressure approach the broker uses to sell the policies.

Former customers

There are many reasons why customers become former customers. They may have been unhappy with the quality of the product, disliked the way the product was sold to them, or found a cheaper solution.

For instance, the owner of a food processing company stops buying packaging from a supplier because he was told that the packages were biodegradable. However, internal testing conducted by the food processing company reveals the packaging does not live up to that claim, despite repeated assurances made during the initial sales contract.

Sorin Dumitrascu

Vanishing customers

Vanishing customers initially seem like excellent prospects. But it soon becomes evident that they're of little benefit to the seller. They often use a false sense of authority that convinces salespeople that the person they are dealing with has control over a large purchasing budget.

For example, Tom works in sales at a software company. He's been in contact with an individual who has expressed interest in placing a large order. Both parties have been involved in intensive negotiations but, suddenly, the buyer reveals that he doesn't actually have the authority to place the order and ceases contact with Tom.

Question

Match each type of customer to its example.

Options:

A. External customer

B. Internal customer

C. High-value customer

D. Repeat customer

E. Former customer

F. Vanishing customer

Targets:

1. A veterinarian buys supplies from a pharmaceutical company

Sales Foundation

2. The quality control section of an appliance company monitors product safety

3. A cell phone manufacturer purchases large quantities of plastic molds

4. Susan purchases groceries in the same store week after week

5. A computer manufacturer finds a cheaper source of semiconductors and stops buying from Jack's company

6. A prospective customer misrepresents her level of influence and abruptly withdraws from the sale

Answer

External customers have no connection to the selling organization.

Internal customers are found within the selling organization.

High-value customers place orders consisting of large volumes.

Repeat customers return to a selling organization because they like the product, customer service, and value.

A former customer is an individual or organization that no longer does business with a supplier due to an issue with the product, or the discovery of a cheaper alternative.

A vanishing customer appears to be a good

Sorin Dumitrascu

prospect but will pull out of the deal.

What do customers value?

Customer value is a loose way of measuring what a customer wants in relation to what the customer is willing to spend. In other words, it's the level of benefit the customer gets from a product compared to its price. From a sales perspective, understanding customer value is essential.

When broken down and analyzed, customer value helps the seller establish customer expectations. It reveals the customer's purchasing behavior and indicates what type of product the customer may be looking for in the future. Customer value isn't based on any particular product – it simply provides an indication of what the customer wants.

Organizations can use customer value as a guide when they are trying to introduce or create value in their product offerings.

Creating or introducing value is a difficult task, as value is a moving target. All organizations seek to add value to achieve a competitive edge – for example, by reducing manufacturing costs, outsourcing, or engaging in e-commerce.

To reach this goal, companies must engage in continuous organizational alignment, assessment, and learning.

Sorin Dumitrascu

When you're finished, select the Compare button to discover if you've listed the three correct sources.

You may have listed a number of sources, but the three main sources of value are the product and services solutions the company provides, the company itself, and the people employed by the company.

The first source of value that customers recognize is the product and services solutions that an organization provides. A customer is very likely to look at the specific characteristics of different products from a variety of sellers.

Customers measure the functional fit of a product to determine whether it provides the best solution. They also consider the added services that bring value to the product. They want to determine if the product has a technical advantage over other similar products.

For example, a buyer chooses an insulation product because it retains more heat and its manufacturer will provide the added service of giving training to the buyer's staff to show them the best way to use and install the product.

The second source of value that customers

recognize is the company itself. Customers choose one company over another for many reasons, such as reputation, financial stability, longevity, size of the company, location, and the quantity and diversity of the products or services offered. Factors such as longevity and corporate philosophy can also affect value from a customer's perspective. For instance, a construction contractor prefers a certain supplier because of its longstanding presence in the community, and its focus on sustainability.

The final source of value that customers recognize is the people. People matter when it comes to selling. If a buyer is worried about the risk associated with making a purchase, it's likely that the quality of the salespeople will be a decisive factor even over price. Buyers want those they are purchasing from to care about their business. Buyers look for honesty, likeability, competence, integrity, business acumen, flexibility, confidence, and trustworthiness in people they are buying from.

Here is an example of a company's staff providing a source of customer value. A public relations firm chooses a slightly more expensive broadband supplier because its salespeople are very competent, likeable, and they made an effort to learn about the buyer's specific needs.

Some buying triggers are rated higher than

others by customers. For example, buyers tend to rate service, support, and product reputation as being more important than product selection, sales competency, and flexibility in negotiating terms.

Because of this value system, it's important that a professional salesperson sells the customer on the selling organization's ability to provide solutions.

Question

Which statements explain what customers value?

Options:

1. The caliber of salesperson can make the difference in a sale where the buyer is nervous

2. A company's reputation and financial stability are important factors for potential buyers

3. A product's technical prowess can be a decisive factor for a customer considering a purchase

4. The advent of e-commerce has negated the influence that people can have on a sale

5. Sales competency is more highly valued than service by customers

Answer

Option 1: This option is correct. Customers rate a salesperson's personal qualities as something they value.

Option 2: This option is correct. A company's

Sales Foundation

reputation and financial stability are valued by customers.

Option 3: This option is correct. When customers look at a company's products and services as a source of value, they look for the product with the competitive edge.

Option 4: This option is incorrect. Although e-commerce is becoming a major part of sales, it hasn't negated the influence that a person can have on a sale.

Option 5: This option is incorrect. Both sales competency and service are valued, but it's service that is more highly valued by customers.

Establishing Effective Communication

Understanding the importance of establishing strong working relationships with customers is essential for any sales professional. To establish good relationships with your customers, you must develop good communication skills. There are two main styles of communication: the leading or manipulative style and the cooperative or consultative style.

You can follow five guidelines to communicate effectively with your customers: listen to the customer's needs, speak their language, establish credibility and trust, let the customer do some of the work, and understand the customer's decision-making process.

Building sales relationships

All sales transactions involve forming some sort of a relationship. You might be phoning a customer to try to make a one-off sale. Or you might be holding detailed negotiations with a procurement manager to secure a long-term sales contract. In both cases, if you want to get the sale, you must establish a good relationship with your potential customer. If you establish that relationship, customers will feel that you understand them as individuals and can meet their needs.

Good communication is essential when building customer relationships. You must develop effective ways to pass information to, and receive information from, your customers.

Communication methods include talking, listening, questioning, understanding, persuading, presenting, clarifying, and building rapport.

In sales there are essentially two main styles of communication: the leading or manipulative style and the cooperative or consultative style.

Leading or manipulative

The leading or manipulative style is generally used by salespeople trying to make a single sale to an individual customer. The salesperson uses techniques that are designed to lead customers to make decisions that lead to a sale.

For example, a salesperson might persistently tell a customer that a particular brand of computer virus software is the best kind. He then immediately asks the customer, "Don't you agree?" Eventually, the customer relents and purchases the product.

Cooperative or consultative

The cooperative or consultative style of communication is suited to situations where long-term relationships are being established. This approach is less urgent and doesn't involve overt pressure being immediately applied.

For example, consider a salesperson taking the time to establish a warm working relationship with the customer. The salesperson displays a genuine interest in the customer's organization and works toward establishing a mutually beneficial arrangement.

Question

Match the examples to the style of communication they represent. Each communication style may have more than one match.

Options:

A. A salesperson in a TV shop designs her pitch so that the customer will develop the same opinion

Sales Foundation

about the product that she has

B. A salesperson selling health and safety insurance policies to corporations begins each sale by researching the possible needs of the company involved

C. A hardware salesperson listens closely to the customer before suggesting a solution

D. A car salesperson repeatedly asserts that a particular model of car is the best in its category

Targets:

1. Leading or manipulative style
2. Cooperative or consultative style

Answer

When salespeople try to push onto a customer, they're using the leading or manipulative style of communication.

When salespeople listen attentively and carry out background research, they're using the cooperative or consultative style of communication.

Communication guidelines for sales

When trying to make a sale, you have to use a communication style that engages and holds the customer's attention. You must also be careful not to annoy, offend, or overwhelm the customer. You can apply a number of guidelines to help you develop communication skills that enable you to foster a good relationship with your customers.

As you may have noted, there're various guidelines that can be used for communicating effectively in sales meetings. Five are covered in this topic: listen to the customer's needs, speak their language, establish credibility and trust, let the customer do some of the work, and understand the customer's decision-making process.

By applying the first guideline, listening to the customer's needs, you can gain a better understanding of the situation your customer faces. This enables you to establish rapport with the customer and start to build a relationship.

When you listen to your customers, you can react appropriately to what they're saying. And you can display empathy and show that you're eager to help them with their situation.

Consider this example. An insurance salesperson uses the initial meeting with a customer to build

Sales Foundation

rapport and learn what the customer and the customer's family need in terms of insurance. The salesperson chats in a polite and casual way asking about the customer's family.

To apply the second guideline, speak their language, you have to know the technical terms and phrases associated with your customers' industries. This can help you impress the customer. For example, a salesperson hoping to sell geological software to a mining company would need to have a basic knowledge of the technical terms associated with the mining industry. The salesperson doesn't have to sound like a specialist, but shouldn't sound like a novice either.

Case Study: Question 1 of 1
Scenario

Nancy is an insurance salesperson. She is meeting with Ross, a supervisor with a mechanical engineering company. She suggests that the meeting take place in one of the company's small meeting rooms. Follow along with Nancy and Ross's conversation.

Nancy: Hey Ross. Thanks for taking the time to see me.

Ross: It's my pleasure.

Nancy: When we spoke on the phone last week

you said your company was hoping to update its current health and safety insurance policy. Tell me more.

Ross: Yes that's correct. My manager feels that the current policy isn't comprehensive enough and wants to negotiate a new policy that provides sufficient coverage. The company employs 50 permanent employees.

Nancy: Given the hazardous nature of the tools and machinery that they use on a day-to-day basis, I guess your colleagues experience a lot of finger and hand injuries. Eye injuries might also be common with little bits of debris flying around.

Ross: Exactly! These are the types of injuries that occur here most often.

Nancy: I have the perfect policy ready for you. We can even finalize the sale today! But first I need some details. What kind of budget has been allocated for this purchase?

Ross: Wait a minute! I'm not in a position to authorize a purchase after just one meeting.

Nancy: Perhaps it's your manager I should be talking to?

Question

How did Nancy conform with the guidelines for communicating effectively during the meeting?

Options:

Sales Foundation

1. Nancy knew what Ross was looking for and for how many people

2. Nancy knew the types of injuries that occur most often in this type of company

3. Nancy demonstrated that she was able to finalize the deal in a fast and efficient manner

4. Nancy wasted very little time in asking how much money the company was willing to spend

5. Nancy showed her determination to find out who was the real decision maker

Answer

Option 1: This option is correct. Nancy listened to her customers needs.

Option 2: This option is correct. Nancy spoke the customer's language.

Option 3: This option is incorrect. Nancy alarmed the customer by doing this.

Option 4: This option is incorrect. Nancy made the customer feel uncomfortable by asking this question.

Option 5: This option is incorrect. Nancy has isolated her main contact with the company and jeopardized the sale.

The third guideline for communicating effectively in sales meetings involves establishing credibility and trust. For a sales transaction to have any chance of succeeding, you need to establish these two important qualities.

You can establish credibility by showing a genuine interest in understanding the customer's problem. And you can then establish trust by proving that you're able to solve the customer's problem.

For example, suppose a salesperson is helping a customer find a fabric for a clothing company. The salesperson could establish credibility by understanding exactly which fabric the customer needs. The salesperson can then gain trust by successfully finding that exact fabric for the customer.

Letting the customer do some of the work is the fourth guideline. If you do all the talking and all the work during the sale process, the client may become disengaged. You should ask customers to carry out little functions so that they remain active and engaged in the process. For instance, a tubing salesperson suggests that the procurement manager of a biotechnology company liaise with the process engineers to see whether the tubing product actually meets the company's needs.

The fifth guideline when communicating with customers involves understanding their decision-making process. For example, a customer buying a new car needs different information at different stages in the sale. In the early stage, the customer needs basic information about the car. In the next stage, more detailed information is required, such as comparisons with other models and performance reports. In the final stage, before deciding, the customer could benefit from an explanation of the benefits of owning the car.

By applying these five guidelines when you're in a sales meeting, you can greatly enhance your potential to make a great sale.

Case Study: Question 1 of 1
Scenario

Mark is a salesperson working for a software company. He is trying to sell a financial management software package to Sally, a procurement manager for a government department. Follow along with their discussion, keeping in mind the guidelines for communicating effectively in a sales meeting.

Mark: Thanks for talking to me today, Sally. I appreciate it. I'm sorry that I can't meet in person. Things are really busy here in the office.

Sally: No problem, Mark. I'm really looking forward to hearing what you have to offer. My department is really struggling to manage a lot of our finance administration.

Mark: Yes, when we spoke last week you mentioned something about that. I don't really remember the details.

Sally: I'll explain it again. This administrative workload is affecting my department's productivity. My colleagues' main responsibility is to process funding applications for agricultural grants. But they can't get enough time to prioritize this task because of this growing finance administration problem.

Mark: Yes now I remember! The software package my company offers will be able to streamline your financial processes and relieve that administrative burden. I don't want to overwhelm you with information at this stage. Its usage would require some initial training from your IT specialists. Perhaps you could contact them and ask if they are familiar with software such as this?

Sally: Yes that's a good idea.

Question

Which aspects of the meeting demonstrated proper use of the guidelines for communicating effectively?

Options:

1. Mark knew what Sally's department was responsible for

2. Mark used industry-specific language that

Sales Foundation

resonated with Sally

3. Mark said he didn't want to overwhelm Sally with information at this stage

4. Mark asked Sally to carry out a task

5. Mark identified Sally's problem and offered a solution

Answer

Option 1: This option is incorrect. Mark didn't speak the customer's language. He couldn't remember what Sally had told him about her department.

Option 2: This option is incorrect. Mark didn't use any industry-specific language that made a positive impression on Sally.

Option 3: This option is correct. Mark showed an understanding of the customer's decision-making process.

Option 4: This option is correct. Mark asked the customer to check if her IT people were familiar with the software he was selling.

Option 5: This option is correct. At the end of the meeting, Mark established credibility and trust.

Building Credibility with Customers

It's important for you to be able to build credibility with prospective customers. This can be difficult because most prospective customers don't look forward to having a salesperson calling on them. As a seller, you have near-zero credibility when dealing with prospective customers.

There are several techniques for establishing credibility that you can use once you've gained access to a customer. You should be easy to talk to; avoid embellishing and using bravado; leverage existing relationships; be honest, humorous, and show courage; use third-party testimonials; and manage the scope of questions.

Engaging prospective customers

As a sales professional, you may sometimes feel that you operate in a very competitive and stressful environment that makes selling a difficult task. To gain an edge over your competition, you must work to build credibility with prospective customers – moving yourself from having near-zero credibility to being viewed as trustworthy and honest. This can be challenging, since prospective customers may not be receptive to your message and may feel your sales call is just taking up valuable time.

Have you ever experienced the frustration of having prospective customers refuse to even meet with you because they only want to deal with salespeople they've worked with before? They may be wary of all salespeople if they've had negative experiences in the past.

Your best chance to establish credibility with customers is to engage them in productive conversations that show you as a salesperson who is clear and honest about what you can and cannot do.

There are several techniques that you can use to establish credibility with prospective customers:
- • be easy to talk to, so that customers feel comfortable,
- avoid embellishing and using bravado,

instead focus on the solution,
- leverage existing relationships that you may have with others in the customer's organization,
- be honest and humorous, and show your courage, particularly if you've made an error,
- use third-party testimonials that demonstrate the quality of your product or service, and
- manage the scope of your questions, depending on the situation.

Question

Harry is a salesperson with a company that provides telecommunications consultancy services. He has arranged a sales meeting with Iris, a purchasing manager for a finance company that has a large customer service call center.

Options:

1. Very credible
2. Somewhat credible
3. Not credible

Answer

Option 1: You say that Harry is a very credible salesperson. Though he did differentiate the type of service his company was selling, he didn't mention any third-party testimonials that could back up his claims. Also, he began the meeting very abruptly

Sales Foundation

without trying to engage the customer.

Continue with the topic to learn more about how to establish credibility.

Option 2: You have rated Harry as a somewhat credible salesperson. He helped establish some credibility by differentiating the service his company was selling. But he didn't come across as being very easy to talk to. He didn't leverage any existing relationships or use testimonials to further establish his credibility.

Continue with the topic to learn more about how to establish credibility.

Option 3: You have indicated that Harry is not credible as a salesperson. Even though he wasn't easy to talk to and didn't offer Iris any third-party proofs or testimonials, he did differentiate the service his company was selling.

Continue with the topic to learn more about how to establish credibility.

Techniques for establishing credibility

The techniques for establishing credibility can be used once you've gained access to a customer. Second chances are very rare in a selling environment, so it's important that you make the right impression and capture the customer's attention. Sometimes it won't be possible to apply all six techniques in a single sales meeting, but try to do the best you can.

The first technique, being easy to talk to, is one of the most important skills you can master.

You should be approachable and accessible at all times. When perfecting this first technique, you should know the terminology of the customer's industry and be willing to listen.

For example, the procurement manager at a commercial printing company was willing to engage with a salesperson from a paper mill because the seller was knowledgeable about the different types and volume of paper required in the printing industry. In addition, the salesperson listened closely to the specific requirements for the manager's particular business.

The second technique is to avoid embellishing and using bravado – instead focus on the solution. Some salespeople rely on bravado and

Sales Foundation

overconfidence to make sales. But if you claim to have the biggest and best product or service, customers may lose interest because they've heard it all before.

You should dispense with boastful generalities and become more specific about what makes your products or services different from the competition's. By being more detailed and focused, you can better match the product's advantages to the customer's situation.

For instance, a salesperson for a custom window company was more successful when highlighting the security features of the windows than when focusing on the claim that the company is the best in the market.

The third technique involves leveraging existing relationships. In this case, if you have a contact you've developed within the organization, you can ask if that individual will provide a personal endorsement. For example, a computer hardware salesperson dealt with the manager at one branch of a bank, and then asked the manager to provide an introduction to purchasing officials in other branches.

Question

Which examples demonstrate the proper use of

the first three techniques for establishing credibility?

Options:

1. Janet has researched her prospective customer's industry and decides to use an official tone in her initial sales meeting

2. A cosmetics salesperson makes sure to address her customers in a friendly and engaging way

3. Sam tells his customers that the software application he is selling is the best in its class and is unlikely to ever be surpassed

4. The bicycle salesperson explains the extra features of the bike that gives it the competitive edge over similar products

5. In a sales meeting Latitia mentions that she has previously sold products to one of the customer's partner companies

Answer

Option 1: This option is incorrect. Janet's choice of tone might discourage the customer from wanting to talk to her. It's better to be warm and approachable.

Option 2: This option is correct. Being easy to talk to is a fundamental way to begin establishing credibility.

Option 3: This option is incorrect. Being

Sales Foundation

boastful about a product's capabilities is an ineffective way to establish credibility.

Option 4: This option is correct. Differentiating the product, rather than embellishing it, is an effective technique for establishing credibility.

Option 5: This option is correct. Leveraging existing relationships is a good way to establish credibility with a customer.

Being honest and humorous, and showing courage is the fourth technique. Humor helps to break the ice and puts your customer at ease. But what if the worst happens and you make a mistake? As uncomfortable as it might be, the best response is to demonstrate honesty and courage. Admit your mistake – being slightly self-deprecating about it – and be confident enough to say that despite the mistake, your product is still the best solution.

Consider Simon, a mortgage salesperson. He quoted an incorrect interest rate to a couple who were shopping for a loan to purchase a house.

Realizing he made a mistake, he contacts the couple and tells them about the error. He jokes that he should have made the calculations using a pencil and paper, instead of relying on a calculator.

After breaking the ice, he reaffirms his belief that the mortgage he negotiated is still a great offer for the couple, even with the new rate. The couple welcomes his upfront and friendly manner, and promises to seriously consider the offer.

The fifth technique is to use third-party testimonials. This is a very efficient way to begin establishing credibility because it allows you to draw on past successes. You can cite instances where your products have been successful in helping other clients meet their needs. The key is to reference very detailed examples that will resonate with prospective customers. Those past successes can really help build your current credibility.

Take Nina, for example. She works as a salesperson for a coolant producer. One of her most successful sales to date was to a company that manufactures engines for yachts.

Her current prospective customer is a manufacturer of outboard engines for dinghies and other small boats. Nina uses third-party testimonials in her sales meeting.

Because Nina is able to demonstrate that her product was successful for a similar company, and because she has testimony from the yacht engine company to prove it, she's better able to engage with the prospective customer.

The final technique for establishing credibility involves managing the scope of questions. The questions you ask can be either open-ended, or closed-ended, but it's important to use the right type of question for the situation.

For example, an open-ended question that's broad in scope is, "What are your company's objectives for the next three years?" This type of question gives the customer the opportunity to talk about many different aspects of the business. You can also ask a question that's open-ended but less broad – for example, "How will the new tax rates affect your company's performance?"

By contrast, a closed-ended question is, "How many people does your company employ?" You would ask this type of question when you require a short and definite answer.

As they say, you only get one chance to make a first impression. So establishing your credibility right from the start is a crucial skill to develop. Put the six techniques for establishing credibility to work for you, and you'll be well on your way to achieving great results.

Case Study: Question 1 of 2
Scenario

Amy is a salesperson with a leather importer. She has scheduled a sales meeting with Sally, a purchasing manager with an upholstery company.

Access the learning aid Leather Sales Meeting to discover how Amy's sales meeting went.

Help Amy gain a better understanding of how to use the techniques for establishing credibility by answering the question.

Question

Which techniques for establishing credibility did Amy correctly use?

Options:

1. Amy used humility and humor in the meeting
2. Amy used third-party testimonials
3. Amy successfully managed the scope of questions in the meeting
4. Amy criticized Sally's competitors
5. Amy offered Sally a discount if she made a quick decision about the sale

Answer

Option 1: This option is correct. When she made a mistake she admitted to it and used humor to re-establish her credibility.

Option 2: This option is correct. Amy mentioned that she had testimonials from another company that confirm the quality of the product.

Option 3: This option is correct. Amy needed some exact information and asked a closed-ended question to get it.

Option 4: This option is incorrect. Being critical

of a customer's competitors isn't an effective technique for establishing credibility.

Option 5: This option is incorrect. Offering a discount on the basis that the customer makes a quick decision isn't an effective technique for establishing credibility.

Case Study: Question 2 of 2

How could Amy have improved her credibility during the sales meeting?

Options:

1. Amy could have given specific details about the performance of her product

2. Amy could have listened closely to what Sally had to say

3. Amy could have leveraged existing relationships to her advantage

4. Amy could have offered to pay for an expensive lunch rather than meet in Sally's office

5. Amy could have said that her company was the number one leather importer in the country

Answer

Option 1: This option is correct. Amy didn't differentiate the product. Instead she referred to it as a general all-purpose material.

Option 2: This option is correct. Amy immediately began the meeting by talking about the price and quality of leather. She should have demonstrated that she was easy to talk to by first engaging Sally in friendly conversation.

Option 3: This option is correct. Amy didn't take the opportunity to leverage existing relationships to her advantage even though she had opportunity to.

Option 4: This option is incorrect. Trying to impress the client in this way isn't an effective method to improve credibility.

Option 5: This option is incorrect. Boasting isn't an effective way to improve credibility.

CHAPTER 5 - Working within the Sales Culture of Your Organization

What is a Sales Culture?
Your Role in a Winning Sales Culture
Personal Accountability in a Sales Culture
How to Excel in any Sales Culture

What is a Sales Culture?

In an affirmative sales culture, the sales function is fully integrated with the company's overall business culture.

There are five basic types of sales culture. In order of the degree of alignment, the types are individual performance, defined outcomes, measurement and evaluation, business value, and revenue growth.

Sales cultures

Every person is an individual with a unique set of work and life experiences. No two people believe in exactly the same things, behave in precisely the same manner, or react emotionally in just the same way. But people's beliefs, behaviors, and emotions are shaped by their environment. People are influenced by the social forces, collective experiences, and demographics of the culture to which they belong.

Although many people think of a culture in terms of a nationality or language, cultural identity is made up of many other components. In fact, a person may belong to many different cultures related to characteristics such as age, religion, special interests, educational level, socioeconomic status, business, or profession.

A sales-oriented business culture is based on the simple concept of optimizing the value exchange.

A sale is essentially a value exchange. Companies provide products to customers and get back value from them. This value is then used to produce further products that satisfy customers' needs and desires.

The sales function is the person, team, or department within the organization responsible for integrating the customer into the value exchange.

Unless an organization is a one-person operation, it will have people, teams, or departments that are responsible for different business functions. These functions can include finance, information technology, human resources, product development, marketing, and sales. Alignment is the degree to which business functions, and the people within them, understand and are working toward the same goals and objectives.

In an affirmative sales culture, the sales function is fully integrated with the company's overall business culture. Each department, work unit, and individual is aligned with sales in a common agenda focused on creating value and meeting corporate goals.

An organization's sales culture also provides salespeople with the ground rules for relationships. This includes both internal relationships – how they operate and communicate with colleagues – and external relationships – how they interact with customers.

Question

Which statement best describes an affirmative sales culture?

Options:

Sales Foundation

1. The sales function is integrated into the business culture and aligned with other departments in creating value

2. The objectives of the sales department are prioritized over those of other functions

3. The sales department is allowed and encouraged to work autonomously to create greater value for the organization

Answer

Option 1: This is the correct option. In an affirmative sales culture, the entire organization is aligned with the goal of growth through sales and profits.

Option 2: This option is incorrect. In an affirmative sales culture, business functions are aligned with common goals and objectives.

Option 3: This option is incorrect. In an affirmative sales culture, the sales department works with other business functions to create value.

Individual performance

There are five main types of sales culture. Each type represents a different sales focus and degree of alignment with the organization. In order of degree of alignment, the types include individual performance, defined outcomes, measurement and evaluation, business value, and revenue growth.

Individual performance

An individual performance sales culture is characterized by an individual approach to sales. It represents the lowest level of alignment.

Defined outcomes

A defined outcomes sales culture is characterized by a team approach to selling. The sales department is internally aligned, but has little alignment with other functions.

Measurement and evaluation

A measurement and evaluation sales culture is characterized by the use of metrics and benchmarking. The sales and marketing functions are aligned, although there may be overlaps or ambiguity in assumptions and perceived responsibilities.

Business value

A business value sales culture is characterized

Sales Foundation

by a focus on market expansion and awareness. The sales and marketing functions are aligned, and customer support is an organizational priority.

Revenue growth

A revenue growth sales culture represents the highest level of organizational alignment. The organization is fully aligned with the sales function and in turn with the marketplace. This culture is characterized by a holistic focus on growth and continuous improvement.

The first type of sales culture is the individual performance sales culture. In this culture, salespeople are focused on individual interests. Success is based on individual performance and sales numbers. This means sales professionals compete not only with people from other companies, but with their own colleagues.

In companies with individual performance sales cultures, organizations prioritize the achievement of high sales numbers by individuals.

Sales professionals are expected to meet those numbers by any means. This results in a "get the sale and get out" mentality, and there's little investment in long-term customer relationships.

Salespeople in individual performance cultures often find it difficult to deal with misaligned processes that conflict with sales efforts. These organizations experience high turnover and burnout rates among sales professionals.

There's also little communication between sales and marketing functions in an individual performance culture. Sales professionals are protective of customer data and information. Marketers may look down on people working in the sales function, discounting their ideas and information.

Because of poor communication and attitudes between sales and marketing, customer expectations for products may be communicated by sales to marketing, but this input is generally dismissed or ignored.

This poor communication results in a lack of alignment with customers in the marketplace because marketing may be sending out different messages about products and services than salespeople are presenting to customers.

Customers whose expectations about a product are not fulfilled are unlikely to continue the relationship, resulting in lower sales and less profit for the organization.

Award Sportswear is a clothing manufacturer. The company's products are distributed to retail stores through sales professionals who work strictly on a commission basis. The company's only other remuneration is bonuses awarded to the top-selling salesperson in each quarter.

Although Award Sportswear products are marketed to teenage customers, its salespeople often concentrate on selling the products to stores dealing with more mature customers.

The organization often experiences a large number of returns at the end of the season, by which time many of their salespeople have moved on to other jobs.

Award Sportswear is typical of an individual performance culture. Sales professionals are paid strictly on commission, meaning coworkers are competitors. Value is assessed strictly by sales numbers and top sellers are the only ones to receive bonuses.

Award Sportswear also suffers from poor communication and misaligned messages between sales and marketing functions. The company markets to teenagers, but salespeople pursue a more mature market.

The company also has a high turnover with their sales professionals. Their high rate of product returns signals that products don't meet customer expectations, meaning lower sales and less profit.

Sorin Dumitrascu

Question

Which are results of an individual performance sales culture?

Options:

1. Low level of communication between individuals
2. High staff turnover
3. No alignment between sales and other functions
4. Marketing and sales relay different messages
5. Sales professionals concentrate on long-term customer relationships
6. Sales professionals cooperate with each other to reach sales targets

Answer

Option 1: This option is correct. In this culture, salespeople are focused on individual interests and there's little internal communication.

Option 2: This option is correct. The misaligned processes that conflict with sales efforts in this culture often result in burnout and high staff turnover.

Option 3: This option is correct. This culture is characterized by an individual approach to sales. It represents the lowest level of alignment.

Option 4: This option is correct. The lack of communication in this sales culture means that marketing and sales often relay different messages

Sales Foundation

about products and services.

Option 5: This option is incorrect. The focus on individual sales numbers in an individual performance sales culture often results in a "get the sale and get out" mentality.

Option 6: This option is incorrect. In an individual performance sales culture, sales professionals are often competing not only with people from other companies, but with their own colleagues.

Defined outcomes

The second type of sales culture is the defined outcomes sales culture. In this sales culture, the organization places value on results produced by the sales department. There are basic levels of support and training for sales staff. The use of consistent sales techniques is encouraged, and there's a recognition of the psychological aspects of selling. Documentation is based on a standard and requires little personalization or revision.

Teamwork is encouraged in the defined outcomes sales culture. The sales department is internally aligned, and there's typically a level of camaraderie and effective communication within that function.

However, this alignment doesn't extend to the rest of the organization. The focus on results in this culture may lead to competition between departments.

Departments don't communicate with each other effectively, and tend to operate independently of one another.

In the defined outcomes culture, the sales department is at risk of falling into a "silo" mentality, where department level agendas are prioritized at the expense of other departments or

Sales Foundation

the organization as a whole.

As long as departments operate in silos, employees have little incentive to share information, collaborate to achieve business objectives, or cooperate to satisfy customers.

In the defined outcomes culture, functional managers are focused only on their own departments or teams. Senior management faces difficulties getting them to think on an organizational scale.

This attitude results in a reactive approach to dealing with issues. Instead of planning ahead or anticipating problems, people cope with issues as problems arise.

This may lead to a system of blame and protectionism, with managers and employees deflecting responsibility for errors and pointing fingers at other departments.

Northglenn Fitness is a large health club and gym. The company is open to members only and the Sales Department focuses on selling memberships based on a standard contract.

Northglenn's sales professionals receive regular sales training, including the psychology of making sales. The company compensates sales professionals through the use of a bonus system. If the team meets its monthly sales target, each person receives a cash bonus.

The company has instituted remedial customer service strategies, but sales staff don't deal with problems. Issues with dissatisfied customers are escalated to the club manager and dealt with on a case-by-case basis.

Northglenn Fitness Club is typical of a defined outcomes sales culture. The sales team is internally aligned and sales professionals cooperate to meet team goals. However, there's little cooperation or collaboration outside the department. Staff is trained in consistent sales techniques and the psychological aspects of selling. The company is also typical in that documentation is standard with little personalization. As well, problem-solving is reactive, rather than proactive, with post-sale issues transferred out of the Sales Department.

Question

Which are results of a defined outcomes sales culture?

Options:

1. The sales team is internally aligned
2. Sales professionals use consistent sales techniques
3. There's a recognition of the psychological aspects of selling

Sales Foundation

4. Issues are dealt with as they occur

5. Problems are anticipated and planned for

6. Sales professionals deal with customer service issues

Answer

Option 1: This option is correct. In this sales culture, the sales team is cooperative and aligned with departmental goals and objectives.

Option 2: This option is correct. In this culture, staff is trained in consistent sales techniques.

Option 3: This option is correct. In this culture, sales professionals understand that selling has psychological aspects.

Option 4: This option is correct. In this culture, issues are dealt with in a reactive manner.

Option 5: This option is incorrect. A defined outcomes sales culture means issues are dealt with in a reactive, not proactive, manner.

Option 6: This option is incorrect. Typically, salespeople don't deal directly with issues that occur after the sale in a defined outcomes sales culture.

Measurement and evaluation

The third type of sales culture is the measurement and evaluation sales culture. In this sales culture, sales value is assessed by analyzing return on investment and performance in relation to competitors in the marketplace.

The measurement and evaluation sales culture represents a higher degree of alignment between people and departments in the organization.

In this culture, departments are more attuned to shared organizational values, and there's an understanding that business decisions need to generate incremental improvements to organizational and operational effectiveness.

Decisions are made based on facts and data gathered from benchmarking and quality improvement methodologies. Documented process standards are used and metrics based on best practices are used as a performance baseline.

The higher degree of alignment in a measurement and evaluation culture means better communication between functions.

Marketing and sales share information and data resulting in products that meet customer expectations. Customer support is a priority for both departments.

Sales Foundation

There's also a proactive approach to problem-solving. Departments such as sales take ownership of issues, and departments cooperate to escalate them as necessary.

Zoflina Healthcare is a national chain of medical facilities.

The organization mainly works with businesses to provide health and wellness services to employees. This market focus is shared by the Sales and the Marketing Departments.

Both functions share data, and the company has instituted a number of methods for measuring and monitoring customer satisfaction with the programs offered.

At Zoflina, new programs are formulated based on customer demand and the cost-benefit to the company. Benchmarking is conducted annually against competitors to keep data current. The company is proactive about customer support. Sales staff deal with issues or make sure problems are escalated to a management level where they can be solved.

Zoflina Healthcare is typical of a measurement and evaluation sales culture. The company makes use of metrics based on best practices to create a good standard of care. It uses benchmarking and quality improvement methodologies to improve processes and to make sure services meet customer expectations. The sales and marketing functions cooperate, and issues are dealt with or escalated to the right level.

Question

Which are results of a measurement and evaluation sales culture?

Options:

1. Quality improvement methodologies improve work processes
2. Metrics based on best practices are used
3. Benchmarking against the competition provides current data
4. Customer support is a priority
5. Sales objectives are prioritized over those of other departments
6. Business performance is assessed through individual sales numbers

Answer

Option 1: This option is correct. In this culture, work processes are evaluated and improved using quality improvement methodologies.

Option 2: This option is correct. In this culture, metrics based on best practices are used as a performance baseline.

Option 3: This option is correct. Benchmarking

Sales Foundation

against the competition provides data needed in this culture.

Option 4: This option is correct. In this culture, issues are dealt with or escalated to a level where they can be solved.

Option 5: This option is incorrect. The sales and marketing functions are aligned in this culture.

Option 6: This option is incorrect. In this culture, performance is analyzed in relation to competitors in the marketplace.

Business value

The fourth type of sales culture is the business value sales culture. In this culture, the organization is focused on market expansion and awareness. It has a high level of alignment between sales and the rest of the organization, particularly marketing.

In a business value sales culture, the organization has developed a business culture that recognizes the importance of the sales function.

Sales and marketing are completely aligned, and trust, rapport, and communication flow are prevalent between the two functions.

Sales professionals develop long-term customer relationships. They recognize the importance of both acquiring and retaining customers, not just pursuing one-time sales.

In the business value sales culture, there's a recognition of intangible value, such as customer loyalty and brand recognition. Because customer relationships are nurtured in this sales culture, the organization can generate more value by repeat sales, and by up-selling or cross-selling more products.

The cooperation and recognition other departments give to the sales function in a business value sales culture generates positive results for the

Sales Foundation

organization.

Improved business processes means quicker and more efficient responses to business issues. A greater awareness of the marketplace and consumer needs stimulates buyer responsiveness.

And sales professionals find it easier to create long-term strategic partnerships with customers.

A business value sales culture recognizes the value of investing in training and development. Sales professionals are expected to learn and become proficient in market-awareness, communication, presentation, and customer relationship skills.

Interswift Mills is a major manufacturer and marketer of a variety of packaged foods distributed through retail stores. The company's major asset is the trust consumers have in its brand.

Interswift's sales and marketing functions work closely together. Both departments receive regular training in market research tools to gauge consumer perceptions about products.

Repeat business is important, so sales professionals concentrate on maintaining long-term relationships with the retail stores that carry Interswift products. These relationships, coupled with consumer trust in the brand, give the company's sales professionals many opportunities for cross-selling and upselling value-added products.

Interswift Mills is typical of a business value sales culture. The company has an appreciation of intangible value in the form of consumer confidence in its brand. The sales and marketing functions are thoroughly aligned, and training and development is prioritized for both functions. The sales staff concentrates on maintaining long-term relationships with customers, and leverages those relationships to implement cross-selling and upselling strategies.

Question

Which are results of a business value sales culture?

Options:

1. The sales and marketing functions cooperate and work toward the same goals

2. Sales professionals concentrate on long-term customer relationships

3. There's a recognition of brand value

4. Customer relationships are ongoing and long-term

5. Customers are receptive to trying new and value-added products from the company

6. Value is assessed mainly through increases in sales

Sales Foundation

7. The organization doesn't invest money in sales training programs

Answer

Option 1: This option is correct. Sales and marketing are aligned in this culture.

Option 2: This option is correct. This culture recognizes the value of developing customer relationships over time.

Option 3: This option is correct. In this culture, there's an appreciation of the value of intangibles such as brand recognition.

Option 4: This option is correct. In this culture, sales professionals concentrate on ensuring repeat business by maintaining long-term customer relationships.

Option 5: This option is correct. Cross-selling and upselling are sales strategies in this culture.

Option 6: This option is incorrect. This culture focuses on customers and recognizes value through market expansion.

Option 7: This option is incorrect. Training and development of sales professionals is important in this culture.

Revenue growth

The fifth type of sales culture is the revenue growth sales culture. This culture represents the highest level of alignment – internally within the sales function, and externally with other departments and functions, and with the marketplace.

The culture of revenue growth represents a fully aligned sales organization.

Repeatable and definable selling processes exist throughout the organization. Support for sales is fully integrated into the business culture and the organization is managed in a systematic and holistic manner.

Technology is leveraged to full advantage, and best practices are institutionalized.

In a culture of revenue growth, all employees understand and are engaged with the company's business culture.

Sales professionals have a clear understanding of the organization's mission, and how their efforts and initiatives contribute to meeting corporate goals.

As well, functional managers in the rest of the business culture are aware of how their departments contribute to growing revenue by supporting the sales function.

Sales Foundation

In a revenue growth culture, the marketing and sales departments are fully aligned. There's full cooperation and communication, but no overlap or ambiguity of work responsibilities between the two functions.

Docusentry Books is a multinational online bookseller. The company uses state-of-the-art equipment and software to coordinate ordering and logistics, and to see sales activities in real time.

The sales and marketing teams cooperate and communicate to reach sales goals. The use of best practices and documented standard operations make sure the responsibilities of the two functions don't overlap.

Docusentry has a low staff turnover because employee engagement is high. Employees understand the organization's culture, and how the sales function supports corporate goals and objectives.

Docusentry Books is typical of a revenue growth sales culture. Sales is fully aligned with other functions, and technology is leveraged to full advantage. Marketing and sales cooperate, but there isn't any overlap or ambiguity about responsibilities. There's a high level of engagement, and employees understand the organization's culture. Good communication ensures there's a clear understanding of sales efforts and corporate goals and objectives.

Question

Which are results of a revenue growth sales culture?

Options:

1. All business functions are aligned with the sales function
2. The organization uses relevant and up-to-date technology to meet requirements and drive sales
3. Employees understand and embrace the organization's culture
4. Sales and marketing functions are cooperative functions with separate responsibilities
5. Employees understand the link between the sales function and revenue growth
6. The sales function prioritizes its department level goals
7. Sales and marketing departments share duties and responsibilities

Answer

Option 1: This option is correct. This type of sales culture is fully aligned.

Option 2: This option is correct. Technology is leveraged to full advantage in this culture.

Option 3: This option is correct. Employee engagement is characteristic of this culture.

Option 4: This option is correct. In this culture, there's no overlap or ambiguity between the sales and marketing functions.

Option 5: This option is correct. In this culture, there's a clear line of sight between sales and corporate goals and objectives.

Option 6: This option is incorrect. This culture is fully aligned and not characterized by siloing behavior.

Option 7: This option is incorrect. There's no overlap of responsibilities between the sales and marketing functions in this culture.

Your Role in a Winning Sales Culture

There are certain characteristics that are shared by winning sales professionals. You'll benefit by being able to recognize these traits in role models at your organization. These traits are reliability, staying power, flexibility, positivity, a good track record, customer focus, a dedication to adding value, and engagement with their products.

Recognizing winning sales professionals

At any organization, the sales function is a powerful driver of revenue. This is because its sales professionals have the closest relationship to an organization's most valuable asset – its customers.

Sales professionals are evaluated on and rewarded for goal achievement. A winning sales professional is someone who can optimize customer relationships to achieve whatever sales goals the organization sets.

Depending on the organization's sales culture, those goals could be related to sales, revenue, market share, customer acquisition, or some other metric.

But what makes for a winning sales professional? Although each person is different, and each company is unique, there are traits that are shared by winning sales professionals in any market. Up-and-coming salespeople can benefit by being able to recognize winning sales professionals within their organizations and by using them as role models, emulating their characteristics.

Role models

As you may have noted, role models are important because they can point you in the right direction, and show you the best way to apply your talent, knowledge, and energy. They're a rich source of experience and knowledge that you can tap into to help come up with productive and creative ideas, strategies, and decisions.

Observing and emulating successful sales professionals isn't about hero worship, or playing up someone's ego.

It also isn't about stealing secrets, or stepping over someone else to achieve your goals. Nor is it about finding someone to do the work for you.

It's about developing the talents and skills you need to be successful in the sales profession.

Observing role models will help you recognize the characteristics that make those people excellent sales professionals.

You'll also learn about how these personal qualities contribute to developing good work habits and effective sales techniques.

And once you've learned to recognize a winning sales professional, you'll be more inspired to become an outstanding salesperson yourself.

Judy works for a food services company. She's risen quickly through the ranks, becoming a divisional sales manager in three years. Judy attributes her success to observing her boss,

Sales Foundation

Marisol. Marisol has both an excellent record of meeting sales goals, and positive relationships with her many customers. When she started with the company, Judy emulated the positive characteristics that contribute to Marisol's good work habits and effective sales techniques, and was soon recognized as a winning sales professional in her own right.

Question

What are the benefits of being able to recognize outstanding salespeople?

Options:

1. You'll become familiar with the characteristics that make for excellent salespeople

2. You can learn a lot about sales techniques from outstanding salespeople

3. You'll become focused on becoming an outstanding salesperson yourself

4. You'll be even more successful than the professionals you're emulating

5. Your job will be easier because you'll be able to find someone to do your work for you

Answer

Option 1: This option is correct. By observing successful sales professionals, you'll be able to determine the positive characteristics that contribute to their success.

Option 2: This option is correct. Once you've identified sales professionals who consistently meets their goals, you'll be able to observe and learn how they do it.

Option 3: This option is correct. Recognizing successful sales professionals can help you focus on emulating their good work habits and relationship skills.

Option 4: This option is incorrect. Stepping over them to achieve your goals isn't the point of recognizing winning sales professionals.

Option 5: This option is incorrect. Recognizing winning sales professionals leads to you developing the talent and skills you need to do a better job, not finding someone else to do your work.

Winning characteristics

Have you ever thought about why some organizations succeed, some fail, and some just scrape by? If you were to observe the business culture of organizations that have achieved true success, you'd find that most, if not all, of them have achieved alignment with their target markets and with their customers' needs and desires. The keys to this alignment are the people who are in direct contact with customers – the sales professionals.

Alignment is crucial to creating sales momentum – the energy that spurs sales professionals and moves the organization toward achieving its goals.

Creating sales momentum isn't just the job of the sales team. In an aligned organization, it's the mission of everyone in the business culture, from the leader through to all the employees.

As a winning sales professional, you'll add momentum with every sale you make. In an aligned organization, this energy ripples back through the organization, stimulating growth, innovation, and engagement.

There are winning sales professionals working in every industry. They have different ages, backgrounds, and levels of experience, and they come from every walk of life. But as different as they are, these winning sales professionals also have several traits in common. These traits are reliability, staying power, flexibility, positivity, a good track record, customer focus, a dedication to adding value, and engagement with their products.

Reliability

Winning sales professionals are consistent and reliable. They respect the valuable time that customers spend with them. They have excellent time-management skills and don't miss appointments. They keep calls or visits short with busy customers, but take time when meeting with customers who need detailed information to make a decision.

Staying power

Top salespeople have staying power. They understand that sales visits, cold calls, and other activities are investments in the future. They don't get discouraged or give up on potential customers after the first rejection. They study the customers and the companies, and improve their approach for the next time.

Flexibility

The best sales professionals demonstrate flexibility when they're making or saving a deal. For example, customers may place emergency orders or make last minute changes. They may require pricing flexibility or have logistical issues that need to be accommodated. Customers remember and appreciate prompt and flexible responses to their needs.

Positivity

Great salespeople show positivity by focusing their thoughts and energy on what they can do to make the sale. When sales professionals are enthusiastic and inspired, it inspires customers to commit to the business relationship.

Track record

The best salespeople respect and enjoy what they do. They have a good track record of success with customers because they like to win the selling game, and happy customers are the way to do that. They love competition, both with other salespeople and with their own past performance.

Customer focus

New customers are important, but good sales professionals never forget about their existing customer base. It can often be more profitable to increase sales to current customers than to invest in pursuing the unknown. Top salespeople keep in touch so they know what motivates their customers' behavior and purchasing decisions.

Dedication to value

The best sales professionals have a dedication to adding value to their customer relationships. They aren't content to repeat the same orders time and time again. Top salespeople understand the concepts of upselling and cross-selling, and how these techniques can be used to increase sales and add value to the customer relationship.

Engagement

One of the most important qualities in a winning sales professional is engagement. The best salespeople believe in their products, their sales teams, and their companies, and they have a desire to share this engagement with their customers. They can make even seemingly mundane products seem interesting, attractive, and desirable.

The sales team at Diallonic Pharmaceuticals has four particularly outstanding salespeople – Song, William, Iris, and Jake. Follow along as they discuss what's important to their success.

Song: I respect my customers' time, so I pride myself on never being late or missing an appointment. Even if my sales calls don't work out, I don't feel I wasted time. I just focus on the next time.

William: The pharmaceutical industry is

changing rapidly. I know it's more work when my customers change their orders, or need products rushed to them, but I understand and I always try to accommodate them.

Iris: I've always been consistent with my customers. In this industry, they have to be able to trust me. And I never neglect my existing customers in favor of new business. My regular customers are a better investment of my time in the long run.

Jake: A lot of sales professionals hop from company to company, but I'm not like that. I can't imagine a profession I'd rather be in, or a line of products that's more important than pharmaceuticals.

Each of the company's four top salespeople has traits of a winning sales professional. Song shows reliability and staying power, and William is both flexible and positive in dealing with his customers. Iris has a consistent track record, and she's very customer-focused. And Jake is dedicated to the company and truly engaged with the products he's selling.

Question

Imagenie Electronics is a large manufacturer and distributor of electronics. Access the learning aid

Sorin Dumitrascu

Imagenie Electronics' Sales Professionals to learn about the company's sales professionals.

Which members of the company's sales team exemplify winning sales professionals?

Options:

1. Binh
2. Carlos
3. Mary
4. Sameera

Answer

Option 1: This option is incorrect. Binh is tenacious and has energy, but his job history indicates he doesn't become engaged with his company or the products he's selling. Also, his persistence could be annoying to customers who don't have the time to deal with him. He should develop his customer-focus and dedication to value.

Option 2: This option is correct. Carlos is a winning sales professional. He demonstrates a positive attitude dealing with customers. His routine produces good results showing he has staying power. He is flexible in dealing with the different needs of customers. And his attention to his customers demonstrates he's reliable.

Option 3: This option is incorrect. Mary has some good qualities, but her pursuit of new customers is affecting the consistency of her sales

Sales Foundation

numbers. She would do better to develop a balanced customer-focus and consider how she can add value to her relationships with current customers.

Option 4: This option is correct. Sameera is a winning sales professional. She has a good track record of being one of the top salespeople at her company. She is customer-focused, maintaining good relationships with existing customers. It's also clear that she is engaged with her job, and her talent for cross-selling shows her dedication to increasing the value of her customer relationships.

Personal Accountability in a Sales Culture

Personal accountability means that you're willing to take responsibility for resolving issues and meeting responsibilities. The three main strategies for taking accountability are to create goals for yourself, have an accountability partner, and form an accountability working group.

Personal accountability

Some of the greatest challenges in business lie in taking personal accountability for the results of your actions. Customers don't want to hear excuses about why a product doesn't meet expectations. Senior management won't be impressed by deflecting blame for not meeting targets.

People often complain about the lack of accountability in their workplace. Sometimes it seems no one wants to accept any blame when something goes wrong.

Personal accountability means that a person is willing to take responsibility for an issue. This doesn't mean that person directly caused the issue, but that he or she is willing to take ownership of the result, and look for a solution.

It also means taking responsibility for meeting sales targets and developing the customer base. If you want to be a winning sales professional, you'll need to be accountable and have an accountability process in place.

Some businesses focus on personal accountability more than others, but by taking charge of your own accountability you'll have an advantage in any sales culture. The three main strategies for taking accountability are to create goals for yourself, have an accountability partner, and form an accountability working group.

The first personal accountability strategy is to create goals for yourself. Goal setting is a process that defines the importance of activities that compete for your time and attention.

When you don't take time to set goals, you're in danger of losing perspective on what's important to your work and career. By tracking your progress toward these goals, you'll ensure your energy is directed toward control of the outcomes in your work.

Properly-set goals and objectives are very powerful motivators. Goals can energize you, focus your behavior, and motivate you to succeed. They also provide a benchmark against which you can assess your performance.

Keep in mind that if something is important enough to be determined as a goal, it's important enough to put in writing.

You should keep track of your goals and your progress toward them. Define the time it should take to reach your goal, and set some progress milestones.

It's important to be specific with goals. Rather than stating "I want to be a better salesperson," you could set an objective. For example, your goal might be "I want to achieve a sales growth of 25% over the next 6 months."

So how do you know where to set the bar for your goals? Your goals should be significant enough to give you a sense of accomplishment when you achieve them. But make sure your goals aren't unattainable. If you're unrealistic about what you can accomplish, you're setting yourself up for disappointment.

Assessing goals

The best way to determine if your goals and objectives are both challenging and realistic is to get a second opinion. Test your goals by sharing them with colleagues, friends, family members, business partners, and other people whose opinion you trust.

The second personal accountability strategy is to work with an accountability partner. One reason many sales professionals fail to reach their goals is because they resist getting support from anyone else. Their attitude is that needing support is a sign of weakness.

But having someone to encourage you, support you, and hold you accountable can be a powerful motivator.

Choosing an accountability partner is an

excellent strategy to achieve this motivation. The role of an accountability partner is simple – to help ensure that you live up to your commitments.

Your accountability partner's role isn't to rescue you, or to do any work for you. Your partner is there to help you do what you've already committed to do.

Your partner provides support so you will become more disciplined, and so more effective in reaching your goals.

But who do you choose as an accountability partner? It should be someone who will challenge you, engage you in the process, and whose opinion and knowledge you trust. It's also important to choose a partner whom you trust to keep your confidence, particularly if your goals involve financial or personal matters.

The third personal accountability strategy is to form an accountability working group. An accountability working group is a group of people who meet regularly to set objectives, provide encouragement, and hold one another personally accountable for achieving goals. They meet to support each other by sharing resources, providing encouragement, and leveraging knowledge.

An accountability working group functions well when members are working toward similar or shared goals and objectives.

People with shared experiences can empathize with you and understand what you're trying to achieve.

Peers also often have experience dealing with productivity issues that can affect your work, such as unconfidence or procrastination.

Group size

The size of accountability groups can vary. The group should be small enough so members don't feel shy or shut out. But it should be large enough to stimulate discussion and provide a variety of opinions. To be effective, there needs to be sufficient interactivity among the group members, and support for each member.

You'll find that others in your accountability group can provide valuable insight to help you deal with issues. They'll also be there to motivate you with success stories of their own.

There are other advantages to an accountability group. You may meet people with whom you can explore ways to partner on projects.

They may also provide you with contacts who have the potential to increase your customer base.

Question

Sorin Dumitrascu

What are some ways you can develop personal accountability as a sales professional?

Options:

1. Create goals for yourself
2. Find an accountability partner
3. Form an accountability working group
4. Don't share goals and objectives with peers
5. Prioritize independence and autonomy

Answer

Option 1: This option is correct. You have to know what you're working toward before you can develop accountability for your actions.

Option 2: This option is correct. Having someone to hold you accountable for your actions can be a powerful motivator.

Option 3: This option is correct. Sharing experiences with a group of your peers can help you gain knowledge and insight into accountability.

Option 4: This option is incorrect. Other people can often provide the support you need to achieve your goals.

Option 5: This option is incorrect. Sharing goals and objectives with accountability partners and accountability support groups are important to motivate you to achieve personal accountability.

How to Excel in any Sales Culture

The five most common mistakes sales professionals make are failure to research the customer, not following up on leads, not prospecting for new customers, taking every sale offered, and fixating on bigger sales.

The seven basic management styles are proactive, animated, forthright, impersonal, controlling, presumptuous, and amateur.

Common sales mistakes

Are you losing sales you think you should have made? Do contacts not return your calls? Do valuable customers fail to do repeat business with you? These issues can arise with any salesperson, but an effective sales professional asks the question "Why did this happen?"

Sales isn't just about what you're doing right – it's also about what you're doing wrong. Identifying and understanding common sales mistakes will help you comprehend their consequences, and avoid these issues in the future.

The five most common mistakes sales professionals make are failure to research the customer, not prospecting for new customers, not following up on leads, taking every sale offered, and fixating on bigger sales.

Failure to research the customer

Before you meet with a customer, it's vital to do your research. If you choose the wrong sales strategy, or offer products that don't meet customer requirements, then you won't make the sale.

Not prospecting for new customers

Sales professionals sometimes become complacent in their work. They settle into a routine

Sales Foundation

and stop looking for new customers. It's important to keep prospecting for new customers if you want to increase sales and replace those customers you lose through attrition.

Not following up on leads

Once you've found some leads on potential new customers, it's important to follow up on those leads. Until you make contact, you'll never know for certain if a prospect might want to do business with you.

Taking every sale offered

Sales professionals don't like to hear the word "no." In fact, it's their business to get people to say "yes." And it's even harder when those same sales professionals have to say the word "no" themselves. But sometimes the wrong kind of sale can be worse than no sale at all.

Fixating on bigger sales

Managing risk is also an important part of being a successful sales professional. There's nothing wrong with devoting time to pursuing a big sale, but not to the exclusion of the rest of your customer base.

The first common sales mistake is failure to research the customer. The sales process is primarily concerned with making contact with customers, demonstrating the features of your products, and converting interest into a firm order.

But you can't sell a product to a customer who isn't interested. Thorough research will allow you to find out what customers want and attract them to your products.

You'll need to consider how you can match the benefits of what you're selling with the needs and expectations of your customers.

Research will also make sure that the customer has the authority to commit to a sale. Consider a luxury car salesperson who spends considerable time with a potential customer only to be told that the customer can't really afford the product. Solving this simple issue could be as simple as asking indecisive customers what their budget is.

The second common sales mistake is not prospecting for new customers. No customer will be around forever. Customers move, go out of business, change suppliers, or no longer have a need for your products.

Successful sales professionals are always on the lookout for new prospects. This systematic process of searching out new customers is known as prospecting.

Make sure you're always informed and up-to-date on industry news. Sales professionals prospect

Sales Foundation

through methods such as personal referrals from current clients, by research in print and broadcast media, by using the Internet, by subscribing to trade journals, and by cold calling.

Consider the sales staff at a large bridal store. Where do you think they might prospect for new customers? They may search the engagement announcements in the newspaper. They could network with other sales professionals such as photographers or cake decorators. They might even attend bridal trade shows, or purchase lead lists data-mined from status updates on social networking sites.

The third common mistake is not following up on leads. It's not easy to face rejection, and many sales professionals avoid following up on leads for this very reason. They make excuses like "I tried that company once before" or "They never return calls" or "It's not worth my time to run after prospects." They forget that every new customer was once a lead.

Consider Mark and Ghita. Both are sales professionals for the same insurance company, and both have access to the same pool of leads provided to them each week. But Ghita makes twice the amount of sales Mark does. Why?

Sorin Dumitrascu

Mark is poor at following up on leads. If he can't reach a prospect right away, he often gives up and moves on. If prospects are reluctant to commit to a sale, Mark blames them for wasting his time.

Ghita is persistent at following up on leads. She keeps trying until she gets a personal reply or reaches a prospect in person. When she senses reluctance from potential clients, she perceives it as an opportunity to customize her offer to better meet their needs.

The fourth common sales mistake is taking every sale offered. An important part of your job as a sales professional is to consciously decide which type of customer relationships you should pursue.

No one can provide all customers with everything they want all the time. Some customers are simply too difficult to serve effectively. Some may be looking for products and services you can't provide. And some customers may cost more to service than they're willing to pay.

Just remember, these issues need to be handled carefully. A spurned customer can become a source of bad word-of-mouth.

Selecting customers

The purpose of developing a customer relationship is to create a mutually profitable

Sales Foundation

relationship. Rather than accept every opportunity that comes your way, you should concentrate on those customers that provide the highest return for your investment of time and money.

Suppose you're a real estate agent selling homes. You may need to turn down clients who have unrealistic opinions about the price they want, or those who want to cover up structural issues with their houses. Or perhaps the costs of selling the house exceed the commission you'll make on the sale. Accepting these clients will set you up for failure, and could seriously damage your reputation.

The fifth common sales mistake is fixating on bigger sales. Sales professionals don't like to admit that they've wasted time, especially with a potentially lucrative customer. But sometimes selling to large organizations is time-consuming and frustrating because decision-making can be slow. Sales professionals also have to balance risk with reward. Putting all your effort into making one big sale can be disastrous if the sale falls through. So can relying heavily on a single existing customer. Maintaining a diverse mix of customers is a more reliable way of maintaining a steady cash flow.

Question

Sorin Dumitrascu

Match each of the common sales mistakes with the most appropriate actions to avoid them.

Options:

A. Failure to research the customer
B. Not prospecting for new customers
C. Not following up on leads
D. Taking every sale you're offered
E. Fixating on bigger sales

Targets:

1. Familiarize yourself with customer requirements
2. Check out media outlets, trade journals, trade shows, and network with other sales professionals
3. Don't negate potential customers before you've checked them out
4. Prioritize accepting customers with the highest return for your investment of time and money
5. Balance risk with reward

Answer

Failure to research the customer means you won't know what customers want or need. Winning sales professionals are prepared to create desire by showing how their products can be of value to potential customers.

No customer will be around forever. Even if your current sales are good, you need to think about

Sales Foundation

the future and not neglect prospecting for new customers.

It's important to be persistent in making contact with prospects. Even if they turn you down, you can use the opportunity to find out what they want from a sales relationship.

Taking every sale you're offered could mean you end up with customers who cost more to service than they contribute financially to the sales relationship.

It can be dangerous to fixate only on bigger sales. The reward may be great, but so is the risk if the sales relationship is ultimately unsuccessful.

Management styles

Few people have as much influence over your sales career as your manager. In fact, the key to your success could lie in the quality of the relationship you build with your manager. By understanding your manager's style, you'll be better able to meet expectations, and strengthen this important business relationship.

All managers are individuals with their own unique personalities and ways of doing business. But most of them fall within seven basic management styles: proactive, animated, forthright, impersonal, controlling, presumptuous, and amateur. Understanding these styles will help you identify and adapt to your manager's way of doing business.

Proactive

Proactive managers are experienced sales professionals who encourage teamwork and prefer to lead by example. They value engagement, honesty, and respect for the customer.

Animated

Animated managers are expressive and people-oriented. They value energy, empathy, and personal flair.

Sales Foundation

Forthright

Forthright managers are direct, honest, and team-oriented. They value loyalty, sincerity, and respect for others.

Impersonal

Impersonal managers are businesslike, calm, and unemotional. They value patience, proficiency, and independence.

Controlling

Controlling managers are detailed, methodical, and process-oriented. They value perfectionism, order, and organization.

Presumptuous

Presumptuous managers are confident, gregarious, and self-absorbed. They value tenaciousness, mental toughness, and personal charm.

Amateur

Amateur managers lack the requisite skills, competence, or emotional maturity to lead a sales force. They value whatever strategies they can find to deflect blame or responsibility away from themselves.

Managers with a proactive style are true leaders. Experience gives them confidence in their own abilities, and they're generous about sharing knowledge with their team members.

Their main priorities are meeting sales goals, engaging their team with the organization's business culture, and mentoring individuals to reach their full potential.

You'll do well with a proactive manager if you show respect for their experience, use them as a mentor, consult with them on strategy, be supportive of your teammates, and meet your sales goals.

Managers with an animated style thrive on the emotional highs of working in sales. They're often enthusiastic, charming, and have a flair for reading other people's emotions. Animated managers are good at motivating their team, and wooing important customers.

They like the workplace to be fun, and they care about what their employees think of them. However, they may have a tendency to hand off dull or mundane tasks on their staff, and may favor team members who are friendly and open.

You'll work well with animated managers if you listen to them when they need attention, are liberal with your praise, and show enthusiasm for dealing with customers and senior staff.

Managers with a forthright style value loyalty to the team and to the organization. They respect hard work, and aren't afraid to give credit where it's due,

Sales Foundation

even at their own expense. They value team success over individual accomplishments.

Forthright managers have an open communication style and don't believe in sugar-coating bad news. They'll go to great lengths to defend their own team, but may resist sharing responsibilities or resources with other departments.

You'll get along with a forthright manager if you're a good team player, and don't grab too much individual credit. You should let them see you working hard and supporting and defending the team.

Question

Match the management styles to the strategies for working with that type of sales manager.

Options:

A. Proactive

B. Animated

C. Forthright

Targets:

1. Use them as a mentor and consult with them on strategy

2. Be open with praise and listen when they need attention

3. Be a good team player, and share credit for successes

Sorin Dumitrascu

Answer

Proactive managers like to share their knowledge and experience.

Animated managers are emotional. They thrive on praise and attention, and need to know you care about what you're doing.

Forthright managers like a good team player. They value team success over individual accomplishments.

Managers with an impersonal style are always in control of their emotions. They often have good administrative skills and do their best to stay out of office politics. They communicate in an efficient businesslike manner, and rarely share any personal information, even with longtime staff.

Impersonal managers are uncomfortable with displays of emotion, and may hide or cover up bad news from their team. Because they dislike giving or getting criticism, it may be difficult to get feedback on your performance from an impersonal manager.

To work with impersonal managers, you'll need to communicate in a calm and rational manner. Keep personal interactions brief. Don't try to bond, or become a personal friend. Update them on progress through short written memos, rather than through personal interaction.

Managers with a controlling style are known as micromanagers. They're the most organized and methodical of all the types of managers. Controlling managers dislike chaos, and are stubborn about adhering to rules and regulations.

Controlling managers tend to focus more on process than on results. They don't put a high value on initiative, and can't bring themselves to trust that you're doing things right. They tend to favor employees who follow their instructions to the letter, even if the results aren't what was hoped for.

To survive working with a controlling manager, use established processes to get things done. Back up your requests with data and information. Get approval before you try anything new and be factual when you communicate. Include times, dates, who's involved, and what the outputs and benefits of your request will be.

Managers with a presumptuous style are the closest real-life type to the fast-talking, flashy-dressing salesmen of the movies. They're aggressive in pursuing a sale, and expect you to have the same drive to win at any cost. They believe in networking, and take full advantage of business contacts.

Presumptuous managers like to talk about their

work and socialize with other sales professionals. They can be difficult to work for because they don't like to listen to other people talk. Nor do they care for weakness or vulnerability. They may be susceptible to errors in judgement because they base decisions on who they want to impress, or to whom they owe a favor.

To get along with presumptuous managers, don't show any fear or self-doubt. Deal with them in person, rather than in writing. Put some time into being friendly, listening to their stories, and socializing if you're invited. They'll respect you if you match their drive and energy in pursuing sales.

Managers with an amateur style are the most difficult types to work with. Sometimes they're inexperienced, or lack the intellectual or emotional skills to be a good manager. They often have an inflated perception of their abilities and tend to blame others when something goes wrong.

Amateur managers are often disorganized, unreliable, and have a low tolerance for frustration. They're the most likely type to have an issue with temper and may tend to bully subordinates by threatening to fire them.

The strategy for dealing with amateur managers is to make a plan to get out of the relationship. Amateur managers rarely have any positive effect on your career. When the time is right, ask for a transfer or reassignment, seek a promotion, or, as a last resort, quit before you're blamed for the amateur's mistakes.

Question

Match the sales management styles to the best ways of working for that type of manager.

Options:

A. Impersonal

B. Controlling

C. Presumptuous

D. Amateur

Targets:

1. Keep personal interactions brief, and keep them updated on progress through short written memos

2. Use established processes to get things done and get approval before you try anything new

3. Don't show any fear or self-doubt, and take time to listen to their stories

4. Ask for a transfer or reassignment, seek a promotion, or quit

Answer

Impersonal managers are uncomfortable with displays of emotion, and dislike giving or getting criticism.

Sorin Dumitrascu

Controlling managers are stubborn about adhering to rules and regulations.

Presumptuous managers don't like to listen to other people talk. Nor do they care for weakness or vulnerability.

Amateur managers rarely improve, so it's usually better to get away from them.

CHAPTER 6 - Developing a Customer-focused Sales Approach

What is Customer-focused Selling?
The Customer-focused Approach
CRM's Role in Customer-focused Sales

What is Customer-focused Selling?

Customer-focused selling is an approach to doing business in which the organization keeps the interests of the customer as its main priority when seeking to sell its products. Being customer-focused can benefit you by increasing your sales and profits, increasing customer loyalty, enabling you to compete on value instead of just price, increasing communication and collaboration with customers, and creating barriers to entry for the competition.

There are several barriers to customer-focused selling. These obstacles include having no understanding of your best customer, little or no customer data, an inability to support your external customer-enabled strategy with an internal customer-focused strategy, and a focus on gaining new

Customer-focused selling

Does this situation sound familiar? Rita is a sales representative for a restaurant supply company. Mario owns and manages a thriving restaurant and had been buying supplies from Rita for several years. Rita could always count on Mario to place a sizable order, but one day, Mario told her he ordered from another supplier. He said the competitor's salesperson had asked questions and learned about Mario's specific business concerns before suggesting products.

Reasons for customers to buy elsewhere

You may have listed price, selection, or availability as reasons for customers to buy from a competitor. While these are all possibilities, it's also possible that customers perceive you or your company as not being focused on their needs and problems. A lack of customer focus can drive customers to purchase products or services from someone else.

Customer-focused selling is an approach to doing business in which the organization makes the interests of the customer the priority when seeking to sell products. Customer-focused companies make clear how their products and services help customers reach their goals, and don't focus only on sales numbers or pricing.

It used to be common that a company's focus was on creating demand and selling to customers. The non-customer-facing services – from human resources to accounting – had no direct or indirect link to the customer. But in a truly customer-focused company, everyone in the organization thinks about customer value.

For example, instead of the head of Accounts Receivable just managing billing and collections, she could focus on the customer by investigating how to integrate the seller's systems with Accounts Payable at the customer's company.

A company that's product-focused attempts to find the most uses, and thereby the most customers, for its product as possible. In contrast, a customer-focused company attempts to find as many products as possible for its customers.

Customer-focused selling emphasizes a genuine dialogue between the salesperson and the customer.

Customers don't want to hear how great your company is or even how wonderful the products are. They want their concerns addressed.

Salespeople need to listen to customers' goals and problems, and not force products on buyers. For example, instead of delivering a generic presentation that focuses on what your company has to offer, have a discussion that explores the customer's needs and determines how your products or services might meet those needs.

Focusing on the customer's needs means addressing the concerns and issues facing each of your customers. For example, when salespeople make a presentation to retailers, they typically assume the buyer is only interested in how well a product will sell. But retailers' concerns aren't one-size-fits-all. One store might need to determine how a product will impact its product mix, another might be concerned with cooperative advertising funds, and a third might be concerned with reliable restocking. Each customer has unique concerns.

Question
What is the correct definition for the term customer-focused selling?
Options:
1. A business strategy designed to reduce costs and increase profits by generating customer satisfaction, loyalty, and advocacy
2. An approach to doing business in which the organization makes the interests of the customer the priority when seeking to sell products

3. A company-wide computer system that focuses on solutions

Answer

Option 1: This is an incorrect option. A customer relationship management strategy – not customer-focused selling – is a strategy that generates customer satisfaction, loyalty, and advocacy.

Option 2: This is the correct option. Customer-focused selling is a business approach that prioritizes the interests of the customer when selling products or services.

Option 3: This is an incorrect option. A company-wide computer system that focuses on solutions can help salespeople solve customer's problems, but it's not a definition of customer-focused selling.

Benefits of customer-focused selling

Some salespeople are content to be thought of as vendors that focus on product details, pricing, and renewing customers' current order levels. But when you focus on the customer, you make the effort to find solutions that help your customers meet their business objectives. Then your customers will have a higher perception of your value. Conversely, the more you focus on product and price, the lower value you'll be perceived as having.

Customer-focused selling will help you have a more mutually beneficial relationship with your customers. This approach may directly benefit you in several ways:

- increased sales and profits,
- more loyalty due to customers perceiving better value and service,
- a new focus on competing on total value to the customer, instead of just competing on price,
- the creation of barriers to entry for competitors trying to gain a share of your market, and
- increased collaboration and communication with customers.

Sorin Dumitrascu

Increased sales and profits

When customers perceive you as being on their side helping them to solve their unique business problems, they will look to buy from you first. This is likely to increase your sales and profits.

More customer loyalty

When the seller and buyer work together, customers will get better service and quality from you and from the whole supply chain. This is likely to lead to customers remaining loyal and becoming long-term purchasers.

Focus on competing on value not price

When you give value to customers throughout their supply chain, price becomes one element in sales, instead of the main driver. This allows you to compete on many more levels.

Creation of barriers to entry

When your company's processes are integrated and working well with those of your customers, it becomes difficult for the competition to take the business away from you.

Increased collaboration and communication

When you have increased collaboration and communication with customers, the sales process will be more efficient and profitable.

For example, consider a manufacturer that is

Sales Foundation

looking to improve its customer-focused selling approach. The Marketing Department was promoting a new product using online banner ads that weren't producing results. After researching the problems facing customers, the banner ads are changed to a downloadable white paper that clarifies the problem, provides ways to solve it, and gives the benefits of the new product. The new campaign produces more qualified leads and results in greater sales.

Question

What are the benefits to you, as the salesperson, of adopting a customer-focused approach to selling?

Options:

1. You'll likely have increased sales and profits
2. Customers will enjoy better value and service and therefore are more likely to be loyal to you
3. You can compete on many more levels than just price
4. You will create barriers to entry for competitors
5. You can ask a higher price for your products
6. You'll see a decrease in labor costs since customers will come to you
7. You can have a more efficient sales process

Answer

Sorin Dumitrascu

Option 1: This is a correct option. When you keep your focus on your customer's problems, they'll be more loyal and are more likely to purchase from you, raising your sales.

Option 2: This is a correct option. With a strong customer focus, your customers will feel like they get better value and service and will likely be more loyal to you.

Option 3: This is a correct option. When customers are happy with the total value you provide to them, they won't just look at price when making purchase decisions.

Option 4: This is a correct option. When customers are loyal and appreciate the value and services you provide, they'll be less likely to need a competitor's product or service.

Option 5: This is an incorrect option. A customer-focused selling approach allows you to compete on more levels than just price, but price will always be part of a purchaser's consideration.

Option 6: This is an incorrect option. Focusing on the customer won't necessarily mean you'll need fewer employees.

Option 7: This is a correct option. With increased collaboration and communication with customers, the entire sales process will be more efficient and profitable.

Barriers to customer-focused selling

No matter how many benefits might be realized, some issues and challenges may deter an organization from becoming customer-focused. Becoming truly customer-focused requires integration of the entire company. If you try to go halfway – for instance, by just training the salespeople – it can cost the company more than just its initial wasted investment. Without a customer focus in all departments, customers will be disappointed. And disappointed customers may lose trust and won't be easy to retain.

There are four common roadblocks that may be barriers on the path to becoming a customer-focused company:
- • no understanding of your best and most valuable customer,
- little or no factual data about customers,
- an inability to link or otherwise support an external customer-enabled strategy with an internal strategy, and
- a focus on the acquisition of customers and not on their retention.

It's vital to find a way around the first obstacle, not understanding your most valuable customer. Experts estimate that 20% of your customer base generates about 80% of the profits. If you don't know who that 20% is, you won't be able to focus on them. For example, if an electronics manufacturer concentrates on retailers, it might be ignoring the end user, its ultimate customer. To overcome this problem, learn all you can about your best customer.

Not knowing about your customer is compounded when you face the second obstacle, having little or no customer data. Often, a company uses only the occasional customer survey to collect data.

In such cases, positive feedback may be noted, but negative data may be ignored. Customers are often unsegmented – that is, lumped into one identical group – and no information about what they want or expect is gathered.

To overcome this obstacle, you should gather customer information and make sure expectations are weighted and ranked. Only then can you make a systematic connection to customer priorities as your company sets budgets and allocates resources.

The first two obstacles also lead into the third – not supporting an external customer-focused strategy with an internal strategy. Internal strategies are vital, since customer focus comes from the inside out. For example, if a manufacturing company wants to better serve its customers but all its initiatives are aimed at reducing time to market, it's never going to be truly customer-focused. Improvement activities should have customer needs and priorities in mind, not what management considers important.

The last obstacle to becoming customer-focused occurs when a company's focus is on customer acquisition rather than retention. For example, if the budgets for sales and marketing campaigns for attracting new customers are much higher than those to retain or expand business with current customers, the company's focus is off.

It's often easier to create metrics for operational activities – such as production deliverables – than it is to create and measure standards relating to quality of service, which is vital to customer retention. For example, a hotel might measure how many rooms are filled each night or how many people order room service.

But to focus on customer retention, it would be better to measure how long it takes to check in or how long customers wait for room service. That would give a better indication of the quality of service customers get.

Sorin Dumitrascu

Question

What are examples of the barriers to customer-focused selling that companies might face?

Options:

1. A company that sells to grocery stores focuses on consumers instead of what the retailers need 2. A manufacturing company gets data on operational efficiency but not on customer expectations 3. A luxury car company wants to provide better repair services, so it initiates cost-cutting measures 4. An online retailer places banner ads with coupons good for a discount on any first-time order

5. A retailer sends a coupon to its existing customers as a thank you for past purchases

6. A software company doesn't understand that employees would like more flexible hours

Answer

Option 1: This is a correct option. If a company's main customers are grocery stores, it needs to understand that and focus on retailer priorities.

Option 2: This is a correct option. The manufacturer is collecting little or no data on customers. You have to know who your customers are and what they expect if they are going to be the focus of your business.

Option 3: This is a correct option. An internal strategy such as cost cutting doesn't support a

Sales Foundation

customer-focused external strategy such as improvements in services.

Option 4: This is a correct option. The retailer is focusing on customer acquisition rather than retention. This is an obstacle to becoming truly customer-focused.

Option 5: This is an incorrect option. Focusing on customer retention rather than acquisition is not a barrier to customer-focused selling. In fact, it's an example of good customer focus.

Option 6: This is an incorrect option. A lack of understanding of employees' desires might be a problem, but it's not an example of a barrier to a customer-focused selling approach.

The Customer-focused Approach

There are five main principles of customer-focused selling. You need to talk situationally with customers – not just give presentations – and ask relevant questions instead of just offering your opinions. You should also focus on the solution your product or service can offer, and not only on your relationship with the buyer. Discuss the product's usage and how that use will benefit the business, without trying to sell only the product's features. Finally, close on the buyer's time frame, not yours.

Principles of customer-focused selling

When you use a customer-focused sales approach, you don't just make a few small changes to your traditional selling technique. It's a whole new approach to sales that allows you to act more as a consultant than a salesperson. But to move from a traditional sales viewpoint to a new way of thinking, you need to leave behind preoccupations with sales goals, fast closes, and quotas.

Traditional selling focuses on convincing and persuading people, and overcoming objections and resistance. If you think about it, it's not really surprising that some people don't have a high opinion of salespeople and assume they're rude or pushy.

After all, what comes to mind when you imagine selling the way it's traditionally been accomplished? You might think of a seller convincing or persuading someone to buy a product, downplaying concerns, and pushing to close the sale.

Now consider the same situation from the buyer's perspective. Many buyers consider salespeople to be aggressive, insincere, and overly familiar exaggerators and poor listeners. Buyers often feel pressured and manipulated into purchases they later regret.

Sorin Dumitrascu

Traditional selling uses the general principles of making presentations, and offering opinions about what you think will work and why you think the buyer should purchase your product or service. Its focus is on forming relationships with purchasers, and it relies on the product line to close the sale on the seller's time frame.

Customer-focused selling, on the other hand, empowers buyers. This type of sales approach helps buyers solve their problems, achieve their goals, or satisfy their needs.

Instead of pushing for a fast close by overcoming a buyer's resistance or not taking "no" for an answer, a customer-focused salesperson will leave if he doesn't think his product or service can help the buyer.

When you move to having a customer focus, you begin to think of yourself more as a consultant. As such, you'll be able to provide your prospects with the tools to help them solve their specific issues.

The principles of customer-focused selling include being able to talk situationally with customers, discussing their specific issues instead of just delivering a generic presentation. You should ask relevant questions, focus on solutions, and discuss the usage of the product. And when you make the sale, you should close on the buyer's time

Sales Foundation

frame, without pressure.

Question

Think about the whole spectrum of selling behavior, from traditional to customer-focused. Where do you think you're located on that spectrum?

Options:

1. Very traditional
2. Some elements of both
3. Very customer-focused

Answer

Option 1: If you have a very traditional approach to selling, ask yourself if you're as successful as you can be, and if your sales interactions are going well. If not, perhaps a more customer-focused sales approach would benefit you. After all, customer satisfaction hinges on meeting needs and expectations, and without a customer focus, you won't know exactly what those are.

Option 2: If you have some elements of both traditional and customer-focused selling, consider the benefits of becoming less traditional and more focused on your customers. When you're thought of as a consultant, your customers will have a higher perception of your value.

Option 3: If you're already very customer-focused, you know the benefits of not persuading or manipulating your customers to buy. When you give them the information to make their own decisions, you empower them and raise their perception of your value, which makes them more likely to keep buying from you.

Talking situationally

Whether you're a traditional seller or already have more of a customer focus, learning to use the principles of customer-focused selling can help generate success. The first principle of customer-focused selling is that you talk situationally and converse with your customers, instead of trying to dazzle them with presentations. Traditional sales rely heavily on flashy slide shows and presentations. Polished graphics, animations, and dramatic effects are often used in traditional selling instead of relevant, situation-specific discussions about customer needs and problems.

You have to be able to relate your product or service to buyers so they can visualize how it will help them achieve goals, solve problems, or satisfy needs. The only way to do this is to have a conversation. When you can talk about industry or business trends and specific issues facing your customers, you'll prove that you know their pain points and have a grasp of their unique situations.

Mario, the owner and manager of a small chain of restaurants, had always ordered his supplies from Rita, a sales representative for a restaurant supply company. Mario recently switched to another supplier because it's more helpful on the issues he faces. The next month, Rita makes an appointment with Mario and is determined to improve her customer-focused sales approach.

Follow along with Rita and Mario's conversation as Rita implements the first principle of customer-focused selling, talking situationally.

Rita: Hi Mario, thanks so much for meeting with me. I know you must be busy getting a strategy together to deal with the new chain restaurant that's being built down the block.

Mario: You know about that? I only just heard myself. Yes, that's going to be tough to deal with.

Rita: It will be a challenge, for sure, but your business is thriving and you have loyal customers. And the regional trend is toward independent restaurants serving locally grown food, which you do so well.

Mario: Wow, Rita, you've really done your homework – I didn't know you knew so much about this area!

Asking relevant questions

The second principle of customer-focused selling involves asking your customers questions about what they need. When you ask relevant questions, you demonstrate your interest in helping them find the right solution. In a traditional approach to sales, the salesperson typically does all the talking, offering opinions about why customers should buy. Instead, buyers should be asked questions that are pertinent and answerable, and that help discover a useful solution. Then they feel you understand their issues and are trying to help, not just trying to make a sale.

If salespeople focus on asking instead of telling, buyers can draw their own conclusions about the product or service being offered. This allows buyers to realize their own visions of their goals or solutions to their problems.

Customer-focused salespeople find out what's important to the buyer first. They don't start telling people what's great about their offering until they've asked questions.

Asking questions allows salespeople to focus on what customers need, not on what they need to sell. For example, if a particular buyer wants to buy a sofa from a furniture store, the salesperson doesn't know if the color, size, style, or price is the most important thing to that person.

Follow along as Rita and Mario continue their conversation about Mario's restaurant and Rita implements the second principle of customer-focused selling, asking relevant questions.

Rita: So do you have any specific business concerns about the competition from the new chain restaurant?

Mario: I do, actually. I don't want to change the high quality of our food, but I'm concerned that I won't be able to compete with their economy of scale.

Rita: You mean that because they buy items in such bulk, their costs are lower, and you might have to buy lower quality items to maintain your prices?

Mario: Yes, that's exactly right.

Question

A salesperson has found out that a manufacturing company is facing problems with multiple legacy software applications in different departments.

Which question do you think best represents the second principle of customer-focused selling, asking relevant questions?

Options:

Sales Foundation

1. "Don't you think you need our seamlessly integrated software solution?"

2. "Do the applications make interdepartmental communications difficult?"

3. "When would you like us to install a new integrated system for you?"

Answer

Option 1: This is an incorrect option. Most people resent being pressured to buy something, and this question is selling-focused, not customer-focused.

Option 2: This is the correct option. Asking a specific question about the applications shows the salesperson is interested, helpful, and trying to discover more about the issues.

Option 3: This is an incorrect option. Asking when the customer would like the new system installed is a thinly disguised way of the salesperson offering an opinion. Traditional sellers often try to project their idea of the solution onto the buyer.

Focusing on the solution

The third principle of customer-focused selling is to focus on solutions. In traditional sales, it's common to think that the seller who has the strongest relationship with the buyer will win the sale. That may be true in situations where the only differentiator is the relationship. But more often, sellers have to help buyers achieve their goals or solve their problems, not just cultivate the relationship.

Customer-focused sales generally target decision-makers, not end users. When you're discussing solutions to business problems, you need to help the right person visualize how your product will solve the problem or satisfy the need.

Traditional selling is focused on relationships and gravitates toward end users because the strength of traditional salespeople typically lies in talking about their products and services. But to solve problems, you need to help decision-makers find the right solutions.

When it's clear your product can uniquely help them, customers recognize value and won't make pricing their only purchasing consideration. When you focus on solutions, you can use your knowledge to improve your customers' situations.

Sales Foundation

Follow along with Rita and Mario's continued conversation as Rita focuses on the solution her restaurant supply company can offer for Mario.

Rita: Mario, I think our new annual purchasing program can help you compete against the chain restaurant's economy of scale.

Mario: Really? How so?

Rita: It's really a new approach. With a purchasing agreement, we estimate your annual need for certain agreed-upon items and give you a bulk rate price. You don't have to take delivery of the whole amount at once, nor do you have to pay for it all up front.

Mario: Wow, I can see how that would help keep my costs down.

Rita: One of our other clients says her costs decreased enough so that she could offer more discounts and specials to her customers.

Mario: That would really help as we go up against a big restaurant chain.

Discussing product usage

The fourth principle of customer-focused selling is to discuss product usage. Traditional selling emphasizes product features, selling points, and the end user's desires. Customer-focused selling is usage- and results-oriented. After discussing why the offering can solve the problem, you talk about how your customers can go about doing just that. After all, if your customers can't figure out how to make your product or service fulfill their needs, it doesn't matter how unique it is.

In traditional selling, the sales force usually doesn't know how products are used or how buyers benefit from them, even though they can discuss all the features and specifications.

In customer-focused sales, you're clarifying exactly how a product satisfies a business need and what return on investment can be expected. So you discuss product usage more with decision-makers than end users. Decision-makers need to know how much something costs to use so they can decide if the benefits are worth it.

Analyzing the situation

As you may have noted, in this situation, no one is showing how the product will help customers

Sales Foundation

achieve goals, solve problems, or satisfy needs. Product usage wasn't discussed, although a lot of excitement was generated.

In a case like this, there may be early-market buyers who are smart and innovative enough to figure out their own product usage, and sales may be OK for a while. But without the ability to discuss how a product is used and how it will help meet specific customer needs, sales will eventually plummet as the market of self-sufficient early adopters dries up.

Now follow along with Rita and Mario's conversation as Rita discusses how Mario could use her restaurant supply company's new purchasing agreement service.

Mario: Am I obligated to buy everything in the agreement? What if I end up needing to use a different product halfway through the year?

Rita: The agreement is flexible enough to accommodate some changes. If there are many items that need to change or if you need significantly less than the agreed-upon amounts, we might have to revisit how much of a discount you get overall.

Mario: That seems fair. But what if I find an item cheaper somewhere else? Rita: Well, you know our prices are good to begin with. And with this program, I can guarantee you'll save at least 10%. An average customer saves 15%, as is shown on this chart.

Mario: Oh, yes. That looks great.

Closing on the buyer's time frame

The final principle of customer-focused selling is to close the sale on the buyer's timeline. Salespeople are always under pressure to deliver revenue on a monthly, quarterly, and annual basis. In traditional sales, closing dates are likely to be based on when the seller needs the order and not on when the customer is ready. In customer-focused sales, decision-makers aren't pressured. Both parties reach a mutual deadline.

When you can carry out the five principles of customer-focused sales, you can compete to win. By establishing a rapport with your prospect you will have a much better understanding of whether or not you'll win the business.

In traditional sales, salespeople don't always ask tough qualification questions, for fear of driving off the prospect. Their emphasis is on quantity of prospects, rather than quality. But you can seldom win sales from unqualified prospects.

In customer-focused sales, you qualify prospects well because you learn about their needs and expectations. As a result, you don't waste their time – or your own – trying to sell them a product or service that won't help them. It becomes a mutual decision when it's worthwhile to allocate resources on your offering.

Follow along as Rita and Mario conclude their conversation about the new restaurant supply purchasing agreement Rita is offering Mario.

Mario: I really do think this a good opportunity that will help me compete with the new restaurant chain moving in. But I can't justify committing all my supply spending dollars right now. I don't even know yet how the opening will affect my business overall. I'm sorry.

Rita: I understand. You've got a lot on your plate right now. Mario, will you do one thing for me?

Mario: Sure, if I can. I'm impressed that you took the time to ask questions and learn about my business concerns. What can I do?

Rita: I'm going to leave this purchasing agreement and the information pamphlet for you to look over. When you've had a chance to think things through, will you give me a call?

Mario: Absolutely! I'm expecting to have early metrics on the new restaurant's impact in a month. If all goes as I think, I'll want to sign up right after that.

Rita: Thank you. I appreciate you meeting with me this afternoon.

Sales Foundation

Question

Raj is a sales representative for a manufacturing company. He's meeting with Tina, a buyer for a large retailer, to try and sell her domestically made products. He's learned that Tina has been having a problem with dissatisfied customers and a high rate of returns of products made offshore.

Match each example from Raj's conversation with the customer-focused selling principle it demonstrates.

Options:

A. "Tina, I'd like to know if you have any issues with the trend toward offshore manufacturing."

B. "So, do you see offshore manufacturing as something that can help your business?"

C. "Our domestic manufacturing has a much lower defect rate."

D. "Our products increase ROI due to decreased returns, and customers are happier."

E. "So you think you'll be making a decision in a week? Great. I can call you then, if you'd like."

Targets:

1. Talk situationally
2. Ask relevant questions
3. Focus on the solution
4. Discuss product usage
5. Close on the buyer's time frame

Answer

Instead of giving a flashy presentation about his products, Raj finds out about Tina's specific situation by getting her to talk about offshore manufacturing trends.

Raj asks a relevant question about the impact of offshore manufacturing on Tina's business, instead of just offering his opinion about it.

Raj focuses on the solution his product can offer to Tina, which is a lower defect rate compared to offshore manufacturing.

Raj clarifies how using his products can satisfy Tina's company's need for a lower rate of customer returns and increased customer satisfaction.

Raj doesn't pressure Tina, but gets mutual agreement to close the sale on her time frame.

CRM's Role in Customer-focused Sales

Customer relationship management is a business strategy designed to generate customer satisfaction, loyalty, and advocacy while reducing costs and increasing profits.

CRM can help you identify and retain customers, manage sales, and customize relationships. It does this by increasing the time you spend with existing customers, allowing for faster customer qualification, providing metrics and data, helping you execute sales faster, and reducing sales cycle time.

Defining customer relationship management

In business, customers are the key to success. To help keep your primary focus on customers, you can use customer relationship management, known as CRM. CRM is defined as an integrated business strategy that helps reduce costs and increase profits through increased customer satisfaction, loyalty, and advocacy. It's a tracking system that helps keep all departments up to date about the status of a customer. CRM allows you to gather detailed information and use it to generate positive outcomes.

In practice, different stakeholders might give you varying ideas of CRM. For example, an executive may think of CRM as a customer-focused business philosophy. An information technology manager may say CRM is a complex process designed to gather customer information. The basic concept of CRM is multidimensional, but overall, the term describes a business strategy, organized around the customer, that helps a company increase its profits.

CRM is essential to customer-focused companies. As a philosophy, it involves identifying, understanding, and better providing for your customers, while building relationships to improve

Sales Foundation

customer satisfaction. CRM helps you understand, anticipate, and respond to your customers' needs.

CRM is a business strategy that makes use of data-gathering software. A company-wide CRM system is critical for managing data flowing to and from the customer at multiple points within the company, and it reduces coordination errors between departments.

But while CRM has technological components, it's more than just software. CRM as a strategy allows you to collate information about customers, sales, marketing effectiveness, and market trends. It allows customer-facing employees to make quick and informed decisions related to sales opportunities, marketing strategies, and competitive positioning tactics.

Benefits of full CRM integration

You may have noted that customers have come to expect seamless, enhanced processes. Customers across many industries have historically complained about a lack of consistency in the information they receive; fully integrated systems address this problem.

Integrating systems across the company enables companies to meet information management and sharing requirements. Without such integration, responding efficiently to customer requirements is much more difficult. Enterprise-wide systems integration also helps ensure a consistent customer experience at every point of contact with the organization.

CRM relies on data and is designed to help track and manage marketing, customer interactions, and relationships across companies both large and small. You can use a CRM business strategy to develop and apply a strategic customer-focused vision, evaluate existing operational processes, and align technological infrastructure requirements with customer requirements.

CRM can maximize customer communications. For example, an electronics manufacturer uses CRM software to maintain a database of which customers buy each product, how often they do so, what options they choose, and whether or not they finance the purchase.

For each customer, the manufacturer can then determine what marketing materials to send, what new products to promote, and what options to emphasize that might help make the sale. The manufacturer would also know whether or not to include a finance package in the marketing materials, and when to target the customer.

Sales Foundation

CRM can also be used to build customer relationships. The manufacturer can remind customers of service dates, notify them of product recalls, and send thank you notices, or even birthday cards.

Question

What's the best definition of customer relationship management?

Options:

1. A business strategy that can reduce costs and increase profits by generating customer satisfaction, loyalty, and advocacy

2. A software application that keeps track of a customer information database

3. An approach to doing business in which the organization seeks to sell products with the interests of the customer as the priority

Answer

Option 1: This is the correct option. A customer relationship management strategy is a customer-focused business strategy that generates customer satisfaction, loyalty, and advocacy. It generally includes using CRM software.

Option 2: This is an incorrect option. While CRM software is generally used as part of customer relationship management, CRM is a business strategy that is more than its technological components.

Option 3: This is an incorrect option. An approach to doing business in which the organization sells products while keeping the interests of the customer the priority is a definition of customer-focused selling, not CRM.

CRM and customer-focused sales

To implement CRM, an organization needs to think of every interaction as focused on its customers. CRM puts the customer first, so being customer-focused is the most important factor in implementing an integrated CRM approach. If you try to adopt CRM but lack customer-focused strategies, you're unlikely

to succeed. On the other hand, if your organization has established successful customer relationships, you can implement CRM to turn those relationships into new and definable customer sales strategies.

CRM puts the focus back on the customer, where it belongs. It combines business processes and technology to create a better understanding of customers. When you track the transactional details of customer purchases, you can discover how to communicate with those customers most effectively. You can also identify new sales opportunities, market trends, and consumer behavior. Truly knowing your customers allows you to effectively target communications to their specific interests. Sales revenue increases, and you create loyal, long-term customers.

There are several ways that CRM supports

customer-focused sales:
- it increases the amount of time spent with existing customers,
- it helps you qualify customers faster and with greater accuracy,
- it provides metrics and data about performance, responsiveness, revenue, and more,
- it allows you to execute sales faster and at a lower cost, and
- it reduces sales cycle time through automated ordering, invoicing, and tracking systems.

Increases time spent with customers

When you streamline information exchange, you can increase the amount of time your organization as a whole spends with each customer. Think about all the employees involved in ensuring customer satisfaction: marketers, advertisers, salespeople, web designers, accountants, customer service representatives, and so forth.

CRM improves customer-focused sales by allowing information exchange and communication. Then every department can work cohesively to ensure customer needs are met. People appreciate a personal approach, and CRM can help you create that approach.

Sales Foundation

Qualifies customers faster

CRM provides data about who your customers are, what they like, and what they expect from you. This allows you to qualify prospects more quickly, since marketing campaigns are reaching the consumers who will truly benefit from your services or products. Furthermore, CRM can help you identify commonalities among clients. With this information, a marketing strategy can become more focused and effective.

Provides metrics and data

CRM provides metrics and data that give you extensive information about performance, responsiveness, revenue per month, customer support, common customer issues, and customer complaint resolutions. It can even help identify weaknesses or common defect points in a product. This data allows you to customize relationships with individuals to provide a higher level of service, helping you exceed your customers' expectations.

Executes sales faster

Using CRM, sales can be executed faster and at a lower cost. When you organize processes and products around customers and collect detailed customer information, you can ensure each customer buys more and remains a customer for life. You can offer your customers what they need, when they need it, and before they have to ask for it, which speeds up sales.

Reduces sales cycle time

The automated ordering, invoicing, and tracking systems of an integrated CRM strategy can reduce cycle time. CRM allows you to manage and track statistics from marketing campaigns, giving you greater insight into new opportunities and approaches, and better-qualified prospects. Therefore, you can reduce the time you spend on the individual phases of the sales cycle.

Question

How does CRM support customer-focused sales?

Options:

1. By increasing the amount of time spent with existing customers

2. By enabling you to qualify customers with greater accuracy and speed

3. By providing metrics and data

4. By enhancing the speed at which sales can be executed

5. By providing automated ordering, invoicing, and tracking systems, which can reduce sales cycle time

6. By decreasing the amount of money a

Sales Foundation

company has to spend on advertising

7. By allowing for greater profits

Answer

Option 1: This is a correct option. CRM supports customer-focused sales because the greater information flow helps increase the amount of time that can be spent with existing customers.

Option 2: This is a correct option. CRM supports customer-focused sales by targeting marketing and providing data that allows you to qualify customers better and faster.

Option 3: This is a correct option. CRM supports customer-focused sales by providing metrics and data that allow you to monitor and enhance sales and customer service performance.

Option 4: This is a correct option. CRM supports customer-focused sales because better qualification and targeted marketing allow sales to be executed faster and at a lower cost.

Option 5: This is a correct option. CRM supports customer-focused sales by using data provided by automated ordering, invoicing, and tracking systems to help reduce sales cycle time.

Option 6: This is an incorrect option. While CRM helps with targeted and effective marketing, decreasing advertising funds doesn't necessarily support or hinder customer-focused sales.

Option 7: This is an incorrect option. CRM is designed to lead to greater profits, but that's not how it supports customer-focused sales.

www.ingramcontent.com/pod-product-compliance
Lightning Source LLC
Chambersburg PA
CBHW031608210526
45464CB00004B/1473